MW00627959

The Vanishing Church

BOB PEARLE

HANNIBAL BOOKS
www.hannibalbooks.com

Published by
Hannibal Books
PO Box 461592
Garland, Texas 75046-1592
Copyright Bob Pearle 2009
All Rights Reserved
Printed in the United States of America
by Lightning Source, LaVergne, TN
Cover design by Dennis Davidson
Except where otherwise indicated, all Scripture taken from the Holy Bible,
New King James Version, copyright 1979 and 1980
by Thomas Nelson Publishers
ISBN 978-1-934749-39-5
Library of Congress Control Number: 2008942815

TO ORDER ADDITIONAL COPIES, SEE PAGE 147

This book is dedicated

to the churches where I have served as pastor:
Hornersville Baptist Church, Hornersville, MO (1980-1985)
First Baptist Church, Clarendon Hills, IL (1985-1990)
First Baptist Church, Portland, TX (1990-1997)
Birchman Baptist Church, Fort Worth, TX (1998 to present)

and to my wife, Deborah,

and to our son, Andrew.

to Him be glory in the church by Christ Jesus
to all generations, forever and ever. Amen (Eph. 3:21).

Acknowledgements

The long process of getting a book in print does not happen in isolation but is a cooperative effort of many people. I wish to thank Blanche Miller for transcribing the sermon series that sparked this project. Blanche was my faithful assistant for many years and left retirement to help me. Gracie Smith was gracious to do transcription as well.

I am eternally grateful for the wonderful staff with whom I am privileged to work at Birchman Baptist Church. They helped shoulder some of my work load so I could finish this project. I particularly want to thank David Hain, Philip Griffin, and Larry Randall for their prayers and support. They are great friends and godly leaders.

In addition to these I want to thank Robert Matz, a seminary student and future leader, for his work in researching the material for accuracy. Paul Kullman, a faithful deacon and friend from a previous pastorate, offered ideas and suggestions as we discussed church matters. Linda Harris, one of God's sweet saints, read and re-read the manuscript for corrections and clarity. The fine people at Hannibal Books are to be commended as well for their professionalism and assistance in seeing this project to fruition.

Last but certainly not the least, I want to thank my sweet wife, Deborah, and our son, Andrew, for their love and support in these years of ministry and particularly in this endeavor. Deborah, a faithful pastor's wife, tremendous Bible teacher in her own right, and an unceasing prayer warrior, was my number-one encourager. Andrew, a seminary student and wonderful son, was helpful in keeping me connected to this generation.

TABLE OF CONTENTS

What others are saying about this book:

With brevity and wit, Dr. Pearle provides the reader with a salient reminder as to the condition of the contemporary church. Dr. Pearle is the rare blend of a scholar's pen with a pastor's heart. As such, every layman, pastor, and academician should be required to read this work. He moves aside the faddish discussions of church growth that appear annually and instead considers the biblical template of a New Testament church which, if heeded by the present generation, can bring the believer's church back to its original roots.

Emir Caner
President, Truett-McConnell College, Cleveland, GA

For those seeking the voice of truth amongst the clamorous chaos of contemporary alternatives, Bob Pearle's trumpet provides a clear and certain sound. In these chapters, each of which could function as a stand-alone sermon, Dr. Pearle weaves through the disoriented threads of modern culture with the powerful needle of Scripture, producing a beautiful tapestry of truth. Peer with him inward into the relationship between God and humanity, backward to the biblical ideal for the missionary community, and forward to a response to contemporary culture that is subtly compelling because of its concurrent orthodoxy and orthopraxy. This book is a reminder as to why Bob Pearle serves as the choice pastor for a growing number of conservative theologians.

Malcolm B. Yarnell III
Director, Center for Theological Research
Southwestern Baptist Theological Seminary, Fort Worth, TX

Foreword

The story of Baptists, from its earliest moments in Great Britain and its genesis in Switzerland and South Germany with our Anabaptist forefathers, is a rich story of ecclesiology. The churches carried the name "Baptist"—a testimony to their practice of believer's baptism by immersion. The title was generated from enemies rather than friends, and, though proudly worn, the title is slightly misleading. The label "Baptist" suggests that churches bearing that title are primarily concerned about baptism. Years ago, Franklin Littell in his famous *The Anabaptist View of the Church* corrected this notion and made it clear that the essence of the Baptist and Anabaptist vision has always been the doctrine of a redeemed church. Baptism was the public testimony of those who were becoming part of the body of Christ—they had indeed died to the old way of life; and, by the power of God's Spirit, they had been born again to walk in a new life with Christ.

How strange, therefore, in the passing of the years that Baptist people would so easily find themselves amalgamated into the larger evangelical world and in so doing forget the incredible sacrifices made by their forefathers who were so committed to this critically important doctrine. In the days of the Reformation and following, Baptists understood that the principle of the union of church and state, adopted by the Magisterial Reformers, was to be rejected all together. Instead they were to favor the autonomy of the church, with a sharp division between the powers of the state and the powers of the church. Never was the church to use the sword but rather to employ the ban redemptively. Never was the state to have any jurisprudence in matters of the church. The state ruled in the sociopolitical realm, but the local church maintained suzerainty in the spiritual lives of its people. Furthermore, unlike the Magisterial Reformers, our Baptist forefathers knew that baptizing infants was not only unscriptural but also dangerous because these infants would grow up in the churches believing themselves to be saved without ever having had an actual experience of regeneration. In turn, the churches would eventually be filled with lost people, who, by virtue of their lost condition, could not carry out the Great Commission of the Lord. Now, in the present era, Baptists have lost their way. The pressure to be at least "evangelically ecumenical" has eclipsed the vision of our founders.

Dr. Bob Pearle, my pastor at Birchman Baptist Church in Fort Worth, Texas, has written *The Vanishing Church: Searching for Significance in the 21st Century*. My hope and prayer is that it will spawn a spate of books on ecclesiology. The uniqueness of our Baptist ecclesiology in emphasizing the believer's church, spiritual responsibility, Christ-like living, and a walk with God in newness of life are the great mandates of the hour for Baptists. If Baptists can recapture their own ecclesiology, as this book makes clear, it will not be in some glorious isolation. Baptists, as they have always done, will revel in both the salvation of genuinely born again people of other communions and in every correct theological statement anyone makes, regardless of his fellowship affiliation. But when it comes to "doing church," true Baptists will want to continue to follow the mandate of Christ in all things, including ecclesiology. So I am profoundly grateful for my pastor's publication, laying out in consistent form the great truths of the New Testament and applying them to the doctrine of the church in the present era. Read this book, and you will become a New Testament Christian.

Paige Patterson, President
Southwestern Baptist Theological Seminary
Fort Worth, TX

Preface

In the early days of America our forefathers came to the new world with the dream of a better life. When they arrived to their destination they began to build their houses and communities. Generally the first public building to be constructed was a church which was built in the center of the community. Every Lord's Day the people gathered to worship God and throughout the week the people came to pray for God's blessings and protection. The church was the center of the community and a mainstay in the lives of the people.

Today, all of that has changed. The local church is no longer the center of community life and, for all practical purposes is vanishing from the scene. Many view the church as outdated and irrelevant—much like the buggy whip and the icebox. What gave the church standing in the community and made her unique was her doctrinal core. Doctrine does not seem to matter anymore and is considered by many to be an impediment to church growth.

When the local church was important, people would "go to church" to worship. Now that the importance of church life is diminishing many people maintain their "spirituality" by going to church in their living rooms in front of their television sets or watching a podcast on their computer screens. The great casualty is the local church is vanishing before our eyes.

Churches that have lost their doctrinal core are struggling with an identity crisis. Their mission and purpose is in danger of being lost due to cultural pressures and historical amnesia. Gustave Flaubert once said, "Our ignorance of history causes us to slander our own times." The effectiveness of a church's ministry is largely dependent upon knowing her confessional identity and staying true to her original purpose. When that purpose is lost or blurred the church loses the full impact she could make upon her community.

King Solomon wrote, "Of making many books there is no end" (Eccl. 12:12). My purpose is not to clutter the shelves with another book but to biblically examine some alarming trends affecting our churches. Some will agree while others disagree with aspects of the book. Hopefully, the end result is we all agree that the local church is indispensible in kingdom work.

This book began with a sermon series I preached to the congregation of which I pastor, Birchman Baptist Church in Fort Worth, TX. My friend, Louis Moore at Hannibal Books, heard the series and encouraged me to expand the ideas and publish them. This work is not an academic treatment on the subject but the passion of a pastor's heart to reclaim the biblical roots of the local church.

Thank you for reading these words and considering them with an open heart and mind. May God bless you and reward you in your service to Him.

SECTION ONE: LOOKING INWARD

Chapter 1

Knowing the Times

The sons of Issachar who had understanding of the times, to
know what Israel ought to do
(1 Chron. 12:32).

Modern-day pastors have been called to declare the Gospel of Christ in what many consider the most explosive time in history. Powerful tides of change are surging across our world. Traditional value systems are crashing while the family is being attacked and redefined, churches and denominations are struggling, and the faith once delivered to the saints is being hurled about by the winds of the day.

During unsettling times in the Old Testament just before David was made king over all Israel, the sons of Issachar had the ability to discern the times and to know what Israel needed. These men knew what action the people of God needed to take. The same need for discernment and wisdom is necessary today to navigate through these uncertain times.

America began as an agricultural society. When the industrial society was born in the 1700s, factories began to spring up and people began migrating from the farms to the cities. Now another major transition is taking place with the demise of the industrial sector and the rise of information technology. The modern age is characterized by satellites, cable television, computers, cell phones, and microwaves.

In the late 1970s Dr. Carl Hammer was the director of

computer science for the Univac Division of Sperry Rand Corporation, now Unisys, when this company was a major supplier of then-called "supercomputers" to the National Security Administration. At that time Dr. Hammer believed almost all of the clerical work in America was already being done by computers. He predicted that "in the 1980s computer business could be the largest single industry in the world, and dominated by American companies."[1]

We live in a time of instant global communication. When President Lincoln was assassinated in 1865, telegraph spread the news across the United States. Five days went by before London received word. When President Ronald Reagan was shot by John Hinckley Jr. in 1981, British journalist Henry Fairlie was at his office within a block of the shooting. Just after the event Fairlie received the news of the assassination attempt when his editor in London telephoned him.[2]

We live in a time of tremendous speed and travel. In 1927 Charles Lindbergh made the first solo airplane flight across the Atlantic Ocean when he traveled from New York City to Paris at the speed of 100 miles per hour. The transatlantic flight took 33 hours and 20 minutes. Today supersonic jets make the same trip in one hour and 46 minutes as they travel at 1,800 miles per hour. That speed is faster than a 30.06 bullet when it leaves the barrel of a rifle!

An economic shift from national to world interests has occurred. The world economy has become more entwined in our national economy. Most of the clothing sold in America is made in China or Taiwan. A large percentage of televisions, electronics, and automobiles, as well as other goods, is imported from other countries.

Society seems to be changing from full-service to self-service. Rarely can one find a full-service gasoline station. Self-service is the rule of the day with do-it-yourself pregnancy tests, electronic banking, and blood-pressure and sugar-level checks.

Even the domestic structure in America is changing. Almost half of all marriages end in divorce. Families consisting of a married couple with children under the age of 18 accounted for 35.7 percent of families in 1997; this was down from 50.1 percent in 1967. The percentage of single-parent families doubled between 1970 and 1990 from six percent to 12 percent of all families.[3]

In society we see a major attempt to redefine marriage altogether. These voices advocate that marriage should no longer be limited to a man and a woman but to any couple, heterosexual or homosexual, where the two persons love each other. Some states have even made homosexual marriages legal.

Theological confusion is running rampant in most mainline denominations; this is leading to these denominations' decline. America's mainline Protestant churches—Methodists, Presbyterians, Episcopalians, Lutherans, Baptists, Congregationalists, etc.—until the 1960s had for generations reported gains. In the middle of that decade, with few exceptions, these denominations began to decline; that decline continues to the present. By 1990 some denominations lost as much as one-third of the membership reported in 1965.[4] The Presbyterian Church (USA) membership peaked in the middle 1960s to 4.25 million members. The 2007 membership report revealed its worst annual membership decline in decades. That same report lists the membership at 2.2 million members—one-half the size it was in the mid 1960s.[5]

In the last four decades six of the mainline Protestant denominations have lost more than five-million members. Yet studies reveal that one-half of the nation's unchurched view themselves as potentially responsive to church if they find one

15

with good preaching and programs for children and if the churches show a concern for them.[6]

In light of the times, what is the church to be doing? She should be giving people true hope. In these times of great stress and anxiety, gloom and doom is heard every day in the news. The church should not echo the despair of secular society but strive to give people hope. She should be proclaiming the grace of God in forgiveness of sin and the believer's victory in Christ. The New Testament is a book of hope based on the resurrection of Jesus Christ. Jesus is alive and offers salvation and hope for people.

In Wood County in the eastern part of Texas is a town named Little Hope. The community dates back to the 1850's. According to legend the town's name originated from the belief that when the local Missionary Baptist Church was organized there in 1881, it had "little hope" of surviving one year.[7]

Many churches today seem to mimic the despair of the age and are rhetorically living in Little Hope. Imagine attending Little Hope Community Church! The name, while novel, obviously communicates failure. A name change would certainly communicate a better outlook—that is, unless the name is changed to No Hope Community Church!

The church, being a family, also should create a sense of belonging. Every person has a need for meaning, structure, and community. Sadly, loneliness is becoming more prevalent in this crowded world. People are living closer together but feel further apart. They seem to be longing for a sense of belonging and that personal touch. Most people like to hear their names spoken and to be recognized by others.

To be isolated and feel unknown, unloved, and unimportant can lead to great personal despair. This is not a healthy condition psychologically or socially. Meaningful personal relationships represent the antidote for such despair and isolation. Who more than the local church can best provide caring fellowship in which people are loved and accepted?

Oftentimes the news media will report a story about a cult's beliefs or practices. Observers are amazed at why anyone would join such a radical or peculiar group. Stories told by former cult members reveal their reasons for joining were because the environment offered meaning, structure, and a sense of belonging. Even though the cult exercised total control over their lives, they experienced a sense of worth and purpose.

Many perceive this world to be a cold self-centered, self-serving, cruel place. Those with that outlook are searching for someone or something to accept them and love them. Christian churches should step up and demonstrate God's love to them.

When Christian churches are faithful in loving people and in proclaiming the gospel, which is the power of God unto salvation, we will be able to observe a transformation in people. The gospel not only is a powerful witness but is able to rebuild in a person's life hope—hope that liberal theology has stripped from many of our churches.

When John the Baptist was imprisoned and awaited execution, he needed clarification as to whether Jesus was really the Messiah. The Baptist sent two men to Jesus asking, *Are You the Coming One, or do we look for another?* Jesus responded to John, *"The blind see and the lame walk; the lepers are cleansed and the deaf hear; the dead are raised up and the poor have the gospel preached to them. And blessed is he who is not offended because of me."*[8] The essence of Jesus' answer was to tell John about His ministry and that when he recognized what Jesus was doing, John would know who Jesus was. That is good advice for churches and believers today.

Just as Christ was ministering to all persons everywhere,

so must the church. George MacLeod, the Scottish clergyman, put it this way:

"I simply argue that the cross be raised again at the center of the marketplace as well as on the steeple of the church. I am recovering the claim that Jesus was not crucified in a cathedral between two candles, but on a cross between two thieves on a town garbage heap; at the crossroads of politics so cosmopolitan that they had to write his title in Hebrew and Latin and Greek. At the kind of place where cynics talk smut and thieves curse and soldiers gamble. Because that is where He died and that is what He died about. That is where Christ's men ought to be and what Christ's people ought to be about."[9]

People are hurting everywhere, marriages are falling apart, drugs and alcohol are destroying lives, violence is growing, and a vast number of people are discouraged. We the church should be ministering with the life-changing gospel of Jesus Christ.

Chapter 2

Deception Alert

Beware lest anyone cheat you through philosophy and empty deceit, according to the tradition of men, according to the basic principles of the world, and not according to Christ (Col. 2:8).

Pearl Harbor is one of the principal naval bases of the United States. It is situated on the inlet of the island of Oahu, Hawaii. This base was attacked by the Japanese Imperial Navy on Sunday morning December 7, 1941. The attack at Pearl Harbor was a complete surprise. Soon after the attack President Franklin Roosevelt appointed a commission to investigate why the attack was a surprise. The United States government had several commissions looking into this during the period of several years. Ultimately, the conclusion was determined that no dereliction of duty occurred by Rear Admiral Husband E. Kimble and Major General Walter C. Scott. They found only errors of judgment. The commission concluded that the warnings that were given were ignored.

Ignoring warnings is fateful—even dangerous. Ironically, however, a whistle-blower or one who seeks clarity and truth runs the risk of being perennially labeled as a *troublemaker*. Many times people are hesitant about taking a strong and courageous stand for fear of how doing so will be perceived. In the Scriptures this is not anything new or even uncommon.

Elijah, for instance, was sounding the alarm to the Hebrew

nation of judgment because the people had sinned against God. They had deserted their own worship of the one true God and had built altars to Baal, one of the chief male deities of the Canaanite people. Elijah was calling for the Hebrew people to repent. He also proclaimed to Ahab, the wicked king of Israel, that no dew nor rain would fall these years except at his word.[10] This naturally led to drought and famine. Later Elijah was instructed by God to meet with King Ahab. When the arrangements were made and Ahab saw Elijah, the king said to Elijah, *"Is that you, O troubler of Israel?"* Elijah answered, *"I have not troubled Israel, but you and your father's house, in that you have forsaken the commandments of the Lord and have followed the Baals."*[11]

Elijah was the one sounding the alarm to the people of Israel. He warned them that if they continued in their sin and waywardness—avoiding the law of God and following other gods—judgment would occur. Who was considered the troublemaker? Elijah, of course.

Jeremiah, the Old Testament prophet from Anathoth, experienced the same fate as did Elijah as a troublemaker. Jeremiah stood for righteousness. He called the people back to God and received all kinds of grief for doing so. Because he was considered a traitor to his country, he experienced attempts on his life. He was even thrown in prison because of his message.[12] Yet Jeremiah refused to back down and continued sounding the warning.

The Apostle Paul and his missionary companion Silas also experienced similar difficulties in the first century. This missionary pair had traveled to Philippi to preach the gospel and encountered a slave girl who was possessed with a spirit of divination. The Apostle, in his Spirit-empowered manner, commanded the spirit to come out of the girl. The girl's owners, fearing they would lose business, seized Paul and Silas and took them to the city officials. The owners accused them of troubling the city. Consequently, the missionary pair was beaten and thrown into prison.[13] How ironic! Those considered by the culture as troublemakers were the people speaking words of life, liberty, and redemption.

Once again the Apostle Paul sounded the alarm. This time the alarm was not sounded to the outside culture but to the church in Colossi. He warned them of certain errors in teaching that threatened the faith of the believers in the church. In Paul's day this error was known as the *Colossian heresy.* Today the same kind of error disguises itself in differing ways in the contemporary church. What happens today is just as dangerous and harmful.

The errors Paul warned about were becoming prevalent in the church. False teachers were attempting to combine Christian teaching with other systems of belief. This syncretism of blending Christian doctrine with other thoughts resulted in a hybrid belief that failed to give the rightful place to the work of Christ. It also stripped the person of Christ of His divinity and His glory. This is the inherent danger of mixing truth from God's Word with other secular philosophies and religions. Interestingly, every feature of ancient heresies in the early church appears in some fashion in the modern church. These endanger the purity of the Christian faith and truth and undermine the church's doctrinal integrity. Paul is sounding a warning to those in the church at Colossi.

While taking the personal risk of being looked on as a trouble-maker, consider this as a warning to the church. In the same way Paul sounded the alarm to the church at Colossi, church leaders should be sounding the alarm to our church today. The modern church is falling prey to at least four deceptions.

The first deception is one of worldly wisdom which is

intellectualism. The Apostle Paul wrote, *"Beware lest anyone cheat you through philosophy and empty deceit, according to the tradition of men, according to the basic principles of the world, and not according to Christ."*[14] Paul uses the word *philosophy*. A philosopher is a lover of wisdom. The general use of the word is good. Paul, however, is using this word in the sense of vain speculation. In this context the word is not being used in a good sense but in a more derogatory sense. Vain speculation covered these false teachers' speculative system which was the essence of their beliefs and also their practical system which was reflected in their lifestyles. Paul is using the word *philosophy* in the sense of how it contained their beliefs and practices which was based on their own rationalism and intellectualism.

We know today what Paul knew then. People practice what they believe. What a person believes does affect how that person lives and what that person does. If people believe that they can do whatever they desire, without recourse, they generally do it. What usually restrains people from doing what they would desire to do? The consequence. Typically people do not want to suffer the consequences that would follow.

Paul is telling the Christians to beware—to watch out for a serious or imminent peril. This warning is being sounded to those in whom he had entrusted his life and ministry. He had invested time in their lives and did not want them to be deceived. His warning was to beware of those who would "cheat" or plunder them—to take them captive through this worldly philosophy. Paul is explaining what he means by *philosophy*. He was not warning against all philosophy but that which is empty—that philosophy which is devoid of the truth. The word is used to refer to things that will not succeed. To paraphrase Paul, he is saying, "Watch out because you will find those who seem so intellectual—so brilliant, but what they are saying is void of the truth. It is empty and will lead you nowhere. It will not succeed."

In this warning the apostle uses another word—*tradition*. At first glance many are immediately turned off by that word. According to many church-growth experts anything traditional is a recipe for irrelevance. If the church wants to be relevant to society and grow, then she must be cutting-edge. What does Paul mean by *tradition*? The word literally means "teaching or ordinance."

He uses the word in two different ways. The first is teaching that the apostle himself received from God and handed down to believers.[15] The second use is teaching that is not from God but rather from people. It is the intellectualism and rationalism generated by human, worldly wisdom. This is the kind of traditionalism in which Jesus excoriated the Pharisees and religious leaders because they had set aside the commandments of God so they could keep their own ideas. Paul is warning the Colossian Christians against this kind of tradition. This is the warning that must be sounded today.

Many evangelical churches in America have been greatly infected by this kind of worldly wisdom. A generation ago the idea began to take root that churches were not very friendly to those "uninitiated" persons and that the church needed to change to be relevant. What emerged is what has been referred to as the "seeker-sensitive" movement. This movement has gained wide acceptance and has been embraced by most church-planters. Though not all that embrace this philosophy are monolithic in their views of Scripture, their methodologies are more pragmatic than biblical. The terminology "seeker-sensitive" is mostly outdated today, but the underlying logic is still the same. Instead of beginning with Holy Scripture and applying it contextually, these seeker advocates begin with human reason and implement it pragmatically.

This is a new approach to church-planting, but it reflects what is happening in the wider culture. David Wells offers great insight into what is happening in the broader culture of which the church is being affected. "What has changed is that now the whole of society has become *avant garde*. The whole society is now engaged in this unprecedented attempt to rebuild itself deliberately and self-consciously without religious foundations. The bottom line of this endeavor is that truth in any absolute sense has been abandoned . . .. Truth is now simply a matter of etiquette: it has no authority, no sense of rightness, because it is no longer anchored in anything absolute."[16]

The methodology used by a church-planter desiring to begin a church would be to first conduct a survey of the community. The questions in this survey would be something such as, "Do you attend a church?" If the answer is *no*, then the questioner seeks to find out why. The answers generally go something such as: 1) "Every one at church is a phony. They dress up simply to show off to others and try to out dress each other. 2) The preachers yell and scream and talk about hell. What they say doesn't help me. I want to know how to manage my money or be a better person. I don't want the preacher to always condemn me and to try to run my life by telling me what I ought to do. Also the preacher talks too much about money. The church doesn't need all those buildings; it should be helping the poor, 3) The music to too dull and boring. I don't know any of those songs anyway. I want something more lively."

With the responses from the residents, the surveyor then asks them, "If you could find a church where you didn't have to dress up—you could go as you are; where the preacher didn't make you feel bad but had beneficial talks; where you would not be asked to give any money and the music would be cool and upbeat, would you come?" At the affirmative response of the resident the questioner would give the person an informational brochure on such a church that will be starting soon in their area. *Bingo!*—a prospect for their church. When the church-starter plans to launch the new church, the worship service is designed with this unchurched person in mind.

This method sounds appealing to get more people into churches, but it is fatally flawed. Who is setting the agenda for the church? Who is dictating the format for worship? None other than the lost and unchurched are! This scheme may build a crowd, but it does not build a church. The entire approach is based on worldly wisdom and the philosophy Paul warns against and not on Scripture. The apostle is warning against this empty philosophy that leads to nowhere.

Some megachurches have begun this way; they are sustained by the same kind of philosophy to which Paul refers. This disease has not just affected church starts but existing churches as well. A great many pastors have moved into existing churches and have created havoc by recommending these churches adopt many of these methods. Pastors, desiring their churches to grow and grow quickly, have embraced pragmatism as their philosophy. They mistakenly believe that the worship and ministries of the church should be formatted to be non-offensive to the unchurched. The environment should be comfortable and non-challenging, biblical terminology should not be used, preaching should address felt needs, and by all means no one should be made to feel guilty.

Many of these leaders proclaim that this generation is different from previous generations and therefore, our message must be adjusted for them. Naturally, the gospel message needs to be presented within the context of culture, whether that is in the first century or the 21st century. No one disputes the fact that society changes and cultures vary, but the basic needs of people have not changed. The Bible declares that we are all sinners and need redemption.[17] The wisdom of this world is an inadequate venue for people to find and maintain a relationship with Christ. Paul declared, *For since, in the wisdom of God, the world through wisdom did not know God, it pleased God through the foolishness of the message preached to save those who believe.*[18] Churches would be better served by pastors who believe and preach, without apology, the whole counsel of God.

Another warning that needs to be sounded to the contemporary church concerns the current trend of churches establishing satellite campuses. This trend tends to franchise the church like a fast-food restaurant chain, placing one church over other churches. What benefits exist to the mother church of having all of these satellite campuses except possibly to gratify the ego of the senior pastor and enhance his prestige in the world? The Free Church movement was based on the biblical model found in the book of Acts where an autonomous church was planted, a pastor was chosen, and the church set free to spread the gospel. What we are witnessing today with the connectionalism of satellite campuses is what led to the rise of episcopacy and ultimately the papacy. The Free Church movement, particularly Baptists, rejected this kind of connectionalism. Yet today some Baptist churches have embraced this connectional concept and still claim to be Baptists!

Another example of Paul's warning that needs to be sounded today is the incessant desire of some churches and denominations to be so culturally relevant that they have adopted "politically correct speech." In their intellectualism and worldly wisdom good biblical words such as *sin, hell*, and *judgment* are to be avoided at all costs. Some of the more extreme forms of politically correct religious speech relate to the Trinity—

that is to the Father, Son and Holy Spirit. Religious feminists seek to amend these references to remove gender-biased language. The feminist trinity is referred to as *Creator, Redeemer, and Sustainer*.

Even our public prayers outside of the local church are to be inclusive and non-offensive according to this politically correct viewpoint. The National Conference for Community and Justice published a pamphlet entitled "When You Are Asked to Give Public Prayer in a Diverse Society." The pamphlet details prayer guidelines for civic occasions. The brochure states, "Prayer in such secular settings can and should bind a group together in a common concern. However, it can become unintentionally divisive, when forms or language exclude persons from faith traditions different than that of the speaker . . .. Inclusive Public Prayer is non-sectarian, general and carefully planned to avoid embarrassments and misunderstandings. On civic occasions, it is authentic prayer that also enables people to recognize the pluralism of American society."[19] The guidelines suggest that "universal, inclusive terms for deity rather than particular proper names for divine manifestations."[20] According to these guidelines Christians should not begin a prayer with "Heavenly Father", for that could be interpreted as sexist, nor should the prayer be made in the name of Jesus, for that could be offensive to others. In other words, a Christian is not to pray according to the guidelines of Jesus but rather to the guidelines of worldly wisdom! Does anyone wonder why the Apostle Paul warns believers against those who would plunder them by this intellectualism that is void of truth and empty?

The second area in which Paul sounds a warning to believers is the area of religious ritual. The first warning was against intellectualism; now he warns against ceremonialism. The dynamic personal relationship with Christ through genuine faith is being replaced with forms, rituals, and ceremonies. Paul writes, *In Him you were also circumcised with the circumcision made without hands, by putting off the body of the sins of the flesh, by the circumcision of Christ.*[21] Throughout the entire writings of the Apostle Paul salvation in Christ alone, by grace alone, through faith alone is advocated. He warns against any other substitutes—even religious ritualism—as a means of salvation.

Ritualism was slowly introduced into the early church and later incorporated into the Catholic Church and adopted into the "high church" form of Anglican worship. The original purpose was to enhance the worship of the individual by giving a visible representation of any invisible or spiritual concept. Opponents of ritualism feared that the actions of the ritual would supersede the meaning that it was intended to convey. Those who supported ritualism believed it was necessary to counteract the secularism encroaching into the church.

Ritualism is rising in the contemporary church and in the strangest places. Paul Thigpen, a Catholic author, writes, "All around the United States nondenominational Charismatics are turning to the ancient forms of liturgy as a way to enrich their worship. In them they are discovering a balance, depth, and rootedness that more spontaneous forms often lack. Some charismatic churches have simply adopted an eclectic combination of practices from the Anglican, Catholic, and Orthodox churches (weekly Eucharist, litanies, clerical vestments, recitation of creeds, etc.) while other groups have begun using the whole order of worship (e.g., the *Episcopal Book of Common Prayer*) or have even joined the Anglican communion or Orthodoxy."[22]

Charismatics, known for their free-flowing worship style, have customarily rejected the traditions and liturgies of mainline denominations. They now are deciding they need a little more ceremony. What is taking place in some charismatic churches is also taking place in some evangelical churches that have historically rejected liturgy. Historically, when churches begin to lose their spiritual vitality, they begin to substitute other religious forms in its place. Their worship may have much activity, but it lacks the power of God. When churches lose the gospel and their spiritual vitality, they ultimately and incrementally replace that loss of biblical truth and fervency with ceremony and ritual. That ceremony and religious ritual now become a substitute for what once was religious authenticity and spiritual fervency.

This metamorphosis can be witnessed today in churches that once were blazing with the gospel and affirmed biblical authority but which now, slowly over time, have abandoned their spiritual heritage. This has resulted in a loss of spiritual power. The unifying factor in these churches now is the religious ritual and ceremony. James Kelly, a member of a group of Episcopalian atheists in Washington D.C., said it best, "We love all the incense, the stained-glass windows, the organ music, the vestments, and all of that. It's drama. It's aesthetics. It's the ritual. That's neat stuff. I don't want to give all that up just because I don't believe in God."[23] What binds these church groups together is not the Word of God, not a vital religion or a personal commitment to Christ, but religious ceremony and ritual.

The third warning the Apostle Paul is sounding concerns mysticism or pseudo-spirituality. Religious mysticism that was invading the early church is raising its ugly head in churches today. Paul says, "*Let no one cheat you of your reward, taking delight in false humility and worship of angels, intruding into those things which he has not seen, vainly puffed up by his fleshly mind, and not holding fast to the Head, from whom all the body, nourished and knit together by joints and ligaments, grows with the increase that is from God.*"[24]

The mysticism invading the early church then and the modern church today is much like Gnosticism—the idea of a superior knowledge of spiritual things—more specifically of angels and things in the spiritual realm which God has hidden from us. Naturally this superior knowledge is advanced under the guise of humility. The apostle, however, reveals it as spiritual pride being vainly puffed up.

Much of this can be seen in the extreme sectors of charismatic churches and leaders. Within those circles are so-called divine revelations and spiritual manifestations that have no biblical support. Yet the congregations are in awe of these things and wholeheartedly follow the leaders.

A recent example is Todd Bentley, the leader of Fresh Fire Ministries. Bentley claimed to have been visited regularly by angels and stated that even Jesus Christ Himself appeared to him. Bentley is known for his body piercings and tattoos and his violent healing techniques that are considered unorthodox even by Charismatic standards. Bentley has even claimed to have raised several people from the dead. Though none of these miracles could be confirmed, that did not prevent the crowds from packing into the Ignited Church in Lakeland, FL. Crowds of up to 10,000 people nightly were reported to attend what became known as the Lakeland Revival. GOD-TV, a religious satellite channel, even pre-empted its primetime programming to broadcast the Lakeland Revival meetings each night.

The events that took place at the so-called "revival" in Lakeland and the things believed by the people attending the meetings would fall under the category of mysticism. The beliefs would certainly not be considered biblically orthodox in any historical context.

As Christians are becoming more individualistic in their

faith and separating themselves from the accountability of a local orthodox church, they are becoming more mystical in their belief system. This can be verified in the common vernacular used today by most people. They generally do not talk about a relationship with Christ but about "spirituality." What does being spiritual mean? It is vague at best and can mean one thing to one person and something totally different to another. This kind of language is becoming more common even in contemporary mainline denominations.

An article by Ruth Armstrong states, "In popular psychology, inner space refers to thoughts, imagery, dreams, attitudes, and feelings, while outer space refers to the external environment. Religion has picked up on this psychology and vocabulary, and sometimes advocates spiritual growth through expansion of inner space, transcendental meditation, self-hypnosis, etc. Such an artificial dichotomy is dangerous."[25] This religious mysticism is definitely from another planet!

The last warning sounded is against baseless beliefs or legalism. Paul states, *Therefore, if you died with Christ from the basic principles of the world, why, as though living in the world, do you subject yourselves to regulations—"Do not touch, do not taste, do not handle," which all refer to things which perish with the using—according to the commandments and doctrines of men? These things indeed have an appearance of wisdom in self-imposed religion, false humility, and neglect of the body, but are of no value against the indulgence of the flesh.*[26]

The imposition of legalism debases the authority of Christ and replaces the law of Christ for law made by people. Such things may have an appearance of wisdom but are folly. This kind of worship is not true worship of God but is arbitrary based on a personal desire. This worship is devised by the self and not by the directives of God.

The two sons of Aaron, Nadab and Abihu, were guilty of such worship and received severe judgment from the Lord.[27] What was their sin? What did they do that was so bad as to lose their lives? The Scriptures declare that they offered *profane fire* before the Lord which He did not command. This profane or strange fire was unauthorized by the Word of God.[28] They had great zeal, but their worship was not according to the Word of God. Carnal passion is no substitute for consecrated praise in the worship of God. He is to be worshiped *in spirit and truth.*[29] The Spirit of God will not be present in worship that is contrary to His Word regardless of how enthusiastic one may feel.

Believers are not left to their own devices in determining how God is to be worshiped. The Bible gives direction. Nadab and Abihu did not follow the biblical guidelines and suffered the consequences. Actually their worship was false worship, even though it was done with great zeal.

When beliefs are not right, worship will not be right. Religious legalism is no substitute for spiritual vitality and merits no favor with God. The errors that are infiltrating the churches, perverting sound doctrine, sapping the church of her spiritual health and robbing Christ of His glory are rooted in bankrupt philosophy. The answer is a return to the sufficiency of the Word of God.

Chapter 3

The Loving Truth

I rejoiced greatly that I have found some of your children walking in truth, as we received commandment from the Father. And now I plead with you, lady, not as though I wrote a new commandment to you, but that which we have had from the beginning: that we love one another
(2 John 4-5).

Sodium is an extremely active element found in nature only as a compound and never as a free element. It always links itself to another element. Chlorine, on the other hand, is the poisonous gas that gives bleach its offensive odor. When sodium and chlorine are combined, the result is sodium chloride—common table salt, the substance that we use to preserve meat and to enhance the flavor of food. Love and truth many times are seen like sodium chloride in that love without truth is deceptive, blind, and naive. Truth, on the other hand, by itself can be very offensive—sometimes even poisonous. Spoken without love, truth can be extremely hurtful. All too often, and particularly in today's culture, love and truth are seen to be mutually exclusive.

People falsely conclude that in demonstrating love, truth must be compromised. Love can be perceived as being soft and flexible and more like sodium, as its qualities play out in life issues. Conversely though, truth can manifest itself as harsh, inflexible, and even poisonous—much like chlorine.

Antisthenes (c 444-365 BC), the third-century B.C. cynic philosopher said, "There are only two people who can tell you the truth about yourself—an enemy who has lost his temper and a friend who loves you dearly." This perceived dichotomy between love and truth can be clearly seen today by the actions of people and proceedings in the churches.

Some churches could be classified as "truth-oriented." These churches emphasize historic Christian doctrine, practice personal evangelism, and place a priority on preaching the Bible, the Word of God. They participate in human-needs ministries but place a greater emphasis on the spiritual needs of people. These churches fall more into the conservative category within evangelicalism.

Then there are other churches that could be classified as "love-oriented." These churches stress social justice and equality for all, self-help recovery groups, and feeding the poor and hungry. They place a greater priority on social ministries and less on the spiritual needs of people. These churches fall more into the liberal category.

Is this divide in churches today a good idea? Are truth and love really mutually exclusive? The Apostle John would say, "No," for he wrote his second letter centering on these two themes of love and truth. His second epistle was written to the *elect lady and her children.* Though some believe John is writing to a specific woman and her children, most think he is writing to a particular local church that he has personified as a *lady* and the members of that church as *her children.*

The gospel of Christ was spreading rapidly in that first century. New church starts were taking place everywhere. These church starts, or house churches, were springing up; the apostles were dying off. However, the letters the apostles wrote instructing these churches were being circulated among themselves. The teachings from the apostles were necessary for these churches to counter the threat of false teachings creeping into their fellowship. Threats to the purity of the gospel and the teachings of Christ were growing. In light of this danger a pressing question concerned the aged apostle. Here was an older Christian statesman looking at the future of Christianity. The pressing question on his mind was how these young churches were to stay strong in the true faith with unswerving orthodoxy and maintain a vigorous spiritual life.

The same question can be raised today within Evangelical Christianity. The threats to the purity of the gospel are just as real today as they were in the first century. Maintaining a vigorous spiritual life without compromising biblical standards is just as pressing. The elder John writes to a local church and instructs her to uphold the loving truth. These are words of truth that need to be heeded today.

We as individual Christians, as well as churches, must place a priority on the truth and procure it. King Solomon, the wisest man who ever lived, wrote, *Buy the truth, and do not sell it.*[30] Truth is the first great priority. It was the basis for John's joy. Truth is the primary ingredient of discipleship. Walking in truth is not an option for us as true followers of Christ.

The truth of God unerringly recorded in the written Word, the Bible, and revealed supremely in the Living Word, Jesus Christ, provides direction for our lives. John however, saw a great danger in that not all who professed Christ were walking in the truth. This is why he rejoiced to know these were *walking in truth.*[31] Some had succumbed to the subtle error of the day. They had been mesmerized by teaching that sounded good and had been infatuated by charismatic personalities.

We see parallels today. In contemporary society and the emergent-church culture truth is viewed as fuzzy, uncertain, vague, and even unknowable. Emergent-church leaders are uncomfortable about declaring any hint of certainty about what the Bible means. Brian McLaren, a leader in the emergent church movement, said in a *Christianity Today* article, "I don't think we've got the gospel right yet . . . I don't think the liberals have it right. But I don't think we have it right either. None of us has arrived at orthodoxy."[32]

Some leaders in this movement believe that the act of preaching no longer is an effective method of communication today. They believe preaching no longer is relevant to a postmodern society. Their justification for this position is their belief that truth cannot be known with certainty. Therefore, they believe for a preacher to stand and deliver a sermon declaring some things as right and others as wrong is ignorant and arrogant on the part of the preacher. These emergent-church leaders believe dialogue is the preferred method of communication in the church. In some churches the office of the pastor has been replaced with a narrator. Addressing the unorthodox views in these churches, John MacArthur wrote, "Uncertainty is the new truth. Doubt and skepticism have been canonized as a form of humility. Right and wrong have been redefined in terms of subjective feelings and personal perspectives."[33]

The church should be *the pillar and ground of the truth.*[34] When believers waiver on the truth and preachers do not declare the truth without equivocation, this is tantamount to *the trumpet* giving *an uncertain sound* (1 Cor. 14:8). No clear distinction is made between truth and error. Decisions then are left to the individual's subjective feelings. The teachings and doctrines of the church have never been left to such flightiness. Christian doctrine is to be based on the truth of God revealed in His Holy Word.

The believer is to search and find the truth of God but also is to practice love.[35] In fact, the theme of love has been fully expounded in the first letter written by the Apostle John. The God who calls us to believe also calls us to love. This love is not based on capricious human emotions but on the human will.

In his second letter the Apostle John defines *love* as obedience.[36] To walk in love is what obeying God means. Love and truth go hand in hand. *To love* in a biblical sense is to walk in truth. To obtain truth is to understand love. The great love chapter in the Bible tells us that love *does not rejoice in iniquity, but rejoices in the truth.*[37] Love and truth are not enemies but dear friends.

We are to walk in truth and to love one another as God has commanded. The elder John makes the practical application by asking, *"For he who does not love his brother whom he has seen, how can he love God whom he has not seen?"*[38] That kind of love is a farce. It is not love, nor is it walking in truth. Love and truth go together.

A failure to love biblically generally points to a failure to know and practice the truth. Biblical love is a strong defense against heresy, just as practicing truth is a strong defense against error. Biblical faith is to be practiced as well as protected, which is why the Scriptures warn against false teachers—deceivers entering into the church leading people astray. These false teachers are referred to as *antichrist*.[39] They are constantly working against Christ. They are deceivers and liars professing to know God, but in reality they do not know Him at all.

These false teachers spread error with a fervent missionary zeal. With great energy they infiltrate the church and cunningly proliferate their error. The doctrine of Christ is not blatantly abandoned but craftily subverted by modern thought. Relevance is the mantra, pragmatism is the method, and novelty is the magnetism.

Novelty—that which is new—is deceptively attractive. Novelty in church growth is promoted as being progressive and advanced in thinking. It is the new way to "do church." The old-fashioned way is presumed to be no longer effective. Everything traditional is out of date and out of touch.

What is new requires great caution. False teachers can sound right and be filled with half truths, yet wrong scripturally. Our faith must be protected by being firmly grounded in truth. This calls for vigilance on the part of believers. Something must not simply sound right but must pass the truth test.

From the apostles' day to the our day, church leaders have called for vigilance. It does make a different what one believes. The elder John tells the church to watch out and to be on guard.[40] They were in danger of losing progress they had made. Some people were advocating all these new ideas yet were not grounded in the Scriptures. Running after novelty would cause them to get sidetracked and possibly even derail.

Complacency is a great danger, especially when error is being attractively advanced by pseudo-spiritual people. Comments made about false teachers by spiritually undiscerning people are, "He's such a nice man; surely he means well," or "She is so sincere in what she says." Academic freedom and diversity are even given as reasons to allow error to be propagated. Yet much more is at stake than sincerity and personalities. The truth of God and eternal salvation are at risk as well as is the life of the church.

Pastors and church leaders concerned about error in the church today do not want to see the church losing ground. All the diligent work of evangelism, of teaching biblical truth, giving counsel to those who are troubled, and sacrificing time away from family would be undercut by false teachers influencing the church in the next generation to turn away from the truth. History is filled with reports of people who chose torture or death rather than to deny the truth. Christian martyrs were valiant warriors for the truth. To ensure their deaths are not in vain, it behooves our present generation to be vigilant for the truth. We should have no doctrinal compromise nor retreat. Pastors should be the lead gatekeepers of biblical doctrine in their churches and should not be conciliatory toward false teachings.

In the summer of 2008 a national denomination met in its annual meeting in Memphis, TN. One of the breakout sessions was led by John Killinger, executive minister and theologian in residence at Marble Collegiate Church in New York City. At this gathering Killinger advocated what the New Testament writers warned the church against. His altered view of Scripture and the role of Christ, his unorthodox position on the person of Christ, and his inability to be certain of anything orthodox put him at odds with the historic Christian faith. Yet he was given a platform in a denomination that claims to be mainstream Christianity! When some questioned the denominational leadership for allowing Killinger to be a presenter, the response was soul freedom of the individual. Church leaders claimed their workshops are a time for exchanging ideas.[41]

No appeasement whatsoever should be allowed toward those who do not hold the doctrine of Christ. No help or assistance of any kind should be offered to them.[42] Rudeness is not being advocated but rather a love of the truth. To extend assistance of any kind to false teachers is not Christian love but spiritual suicide and exposes the church to error, which will undermine the faith once for all delivered to the saints.

False teachers should not be welcomed into the churches. They are not to be given a platform to speak to the congregation or even endorsed by those within the church, particularly by church leaders.

After one particularly humiliating defeat in a football game, the legendary coach Vince Lombardi is reported to have started the next day's practice in an unusual way. "Gentlemen, this is a football" he said as he held up the football for all to see. His point was obvious. If his football team was to win games, the players would have to master the basics.

The admonition in Scripture given by the Apostle John in his later years is for believers to understand the basics of the Christian life. Truth is priority. God is a God of Truth. He cannot lie. His Word is Truth. Love is to be practiced. God is also a God of Love. Truth and love are not adversaries but friends.

SECTION TWO: LOOKING BACKWARD

Chapter 4

The Church of the Living God

*. . . but if I am delayed, I write so that you may know how you
ought to conduct yourself in the house of God, which is the
church of the living God, the pillar and ground of the truth*
(1 Tim. 3:15).

An identity crisis is confronting American Christianity
today. This crisis is a failure to understand what the church
really is—to understand her purpose and mission. Almost two
decades ago William Willimon wrote in *The Christian Century*
magazine an article about Christians and Western culture.[43]
The article talked about the relationship of the Christian faith
and Western culture. It said that once Christianity was culturally established, but now it is clearly disestablished from our
culture. This disestablishment of Christianity from Western
culture has helped liberalism by keeping people vaguely relat-
ed to the church.

From a liberal perspective, Christian eschatology has been
translated into Marxist revolutionary causes. This is the basis
for Liberation Theology. Liberalism seems to be the spring-
board for many unorthodox movements within Christianity.
Salvation today has been translated into "self-fulfillment" by
less-than-orthodox teachers. Denominational bishops speak on
social issues to convince society that the church really cares
about what society cares about and in the same way society
cares. Willimon states, "We keep people interested in the
church even though they no longer worship its God."[44]

For numerous reasons, American Christianity is in crisis. Many Americans simply think of the church as a "place to go" to merit some standing in their community or to get married or for some other social function. Others view the church as the fountainhead to satisfy their own particular felt needs. The church is the place where their selfish desires and felt needs get center stage. The autonomous self is maximized.

Sociologist Robert Bella refers to this as "radical individualism."[45] He says that radical individualism is defining the reality of American life. Americans are so self-absorbed in our own thinking and in our own frames of reference that we see everything in terms of how to satisfy our own personal wants and desires. This individualism has even invaded the church and is shaping our ideas about religion.

A few years ago a newspaper advertisement for a golf course in Wisconsin offered Sunday-morning golfers combined worship on the green at the Nine Springs Golf Course at 8 a.m. to 8:20 a.m. Golfers could dress casually, attend a 20-minute service "worshiping God on the green", and then get on with their golf games!

The *Rapid City Journal* carried an article about a church in Greenwich, NJ. The piece notes that the church's minister is trying a new way to draw people into the fold—an express 22-minute service that provides all the spirituality of the regular liturgy "in half the time." The shortened version "eliminates sermons and sacraments." This true version of the "Lite" church "includes a greeting, apology for sins, prayer, and an interpretation of the weekly Bible reading."

George MacLeod said, "The greatest criticism of the church today is that no one wants to persecute it because there is nothing very much to persecute it about." What an indictment on American Christianity! The picture of the church painted by the newspaper advertisements may aptly reflect a great segment of the churches in America today, but they certainly do not resemble God's distinct picture of the New Testament churches.

What kind of picture does the New Testament paint when teaching about the church? A good starting point is beginning with a proper definition. The word *church* in the Bible is a translation of the Greek word *ekklesia*. This word had pre-Christian origins. The ancient Greeks referred to a public assembly, typically an assembly of citizens, for the purpose of dealing with matters of public concerns.

Luke, writing in the book of Acts, tells about the Apostle Paul's time in the city of Ephesus where a riot was created by a silversmith named Demetrius.[46] This man stirred up the city against Paul because people were being converted to Christ by Paul's preaching. These new converts were forsaking their occult past—even burning their magic books and silver shrines to Diana for all to see. Demetrius, a wealthy businessman, was fearful of losing business and therefore created a commotion to get rid of Paul. The frenzied crowd seized Paul's travel companions and took them to the theater. This gathered group in the theater is referred to as an *ekklesia*.[47]

The people went from their homes, businesses, and neighborhoods to gather in the theater to determine what to do with these Gospel preachers. Though it was an unlawful gathering (*ekklesia*)[48], at the conclusion of the matter the magistrate dismissed the assembly (*ekklesia*)[49] and everyone left.

The Septuagint (LXX), the Greek translation of the Old Testament, also translates *ekklesia* as "assembly" or "congregation." When Moses led the children of Israel out of Egyptian bondage, they crossed the Red Sea and wandered in the wilderness because of their unbelief. The children of Israel, gathered in the wilderness, were referred to as an *ekklesia* or "congregation in the wilderness."[50] When King David writes in the Psalms, quoted in the New Testament by the writer of the book of Hebrews, David declares, "In the midst of the assembly I will praise You."[51] Again the LXX translates *ekklesia* as assembly or congregation of God's people.

The differing uses of this word are clearly seen in the Scripture. It is used in a secular sense in Acts about events in the city of Ephesus, in a religious sense with the children of Israel gathered together in the wilderness, and by King David when the people of God are gathered together in worship.

The Greek word *ekklesia* denotes an assembly and differs from the English word *church*. The word *church* is often used to refer to the house or building where the assembling takes place. In the New Testament *ekklesia* does not denote the house or building in which the worshipers gather. It always refers to those people who are gathered together, not to the bricks and sticks of the building, but always to the people. Today's vernacular is sometimes confusing, because church is used more often in terms of the structure and not the people.

The word *synagogue* is used in the Bible in a dual sense. It refers to the worshipers but also to the house in which the worshipers assemble. Luke uses it in this two-fold sense.[52] When a centurion's servant was sick, Jewish elders were sent to try to convince Jesus to heal this servant because the centurion was deserving. He had built a synagogue for them—that is, a house where they could go and worship. Here the word *synagogue* refers to the building. This distinction can be seen in Paul's first letter to Timothy "that you may know how you ought to conduct yourself in the house (*oikos*) of God, which is the church (*ekklesia*) of the living God, the pillar and ground of the truth."[53] The house refers to the building and the church (*ekklesia*) refers to people gathered in the building.

Ekklesia is a compound word from *ek* meaning "out" and a derivative of *kaleo* meaning "call." The assembly or congregation is defined as those who are called out from their homes to gather in a certain place for a specific purpose. Religiously these people are called out from their homes to gather in a particular locale for worship. This is the biblical picture of the New Testament congregation or church. *Ekklesia* is used almost 120 times in the New Testament. All but about 15 of them refer to a local, particular, identifiable congregation or a group of churches.

The New Testament speaks of churches with a place of meeting specified. It mentions the church at Jerusalem,[54] the church at Antioch,[55] the church at Corinth,[56] etc. Each of these churches met in particular locations and could be identified. The parallel today would be the First Baptist Church or Second Presbyterian Church or Central Community Church in a certain city. The believers in those congregations would leave their homes and gather in a particular place at a specified time to worship God. Someone wanting to visit those churches would know where to go and when to be there.

When the writers of the New Testament referred to several congregations in a region, the plural form was used. For example, the churches throughout all Judea, Galilee, and Samaria,[57] the churches of Asia,[58] the churches of Galatia.[59] Each of the local churches was distinct from each other. They met at different places and different times under their own leadership. Elders or pastors were appointed in every church.[60] The churches did not have one single pastor over all of the believers. When the Apostle Paul left Macedonia and also needed assistance in Thessalonica, the only church that supported him was in Philippi.[61] This suggests that each church is autonomous in what ministries she supports.

The 15 times *ekklesia* is not used in a local sense, it is used in a universal sense. More than half of those uses are found exclusively in the book of Ephesians. John Dagg, an early president of Mercer University and significant Baptist theologian, defined the *universal church* as "the whole company of those that are saved by Christ."[62] This refers to all who have ever been redeemed by Christ—past, present, and future. In the New Testament we see a distinction between the local and universal church with the primary reference being the local church.

B. H. Carroll, the founder and first president of Southwestern Baptist Theological Seminary, taught that the word *church* is used in the New Testament in three distinct senses: 1. Abstractly as an institution (Matt. 16:18). 2. A particular congregation at one place (1 Cor 1:2). 3. All the redeemed conceived of as a unit and glorified as a bride or city (Eph 5:25-27 and Rev 21:9-10).[63]

Some have in error referred to the *universal church* as the *invisible church*. This is a concept foreign to the New Testament and actually contradicts the meaning of *ekklesia* all together. How can an invisible assembly of believers exist? Robert Saucy weighs in here by noting that an invisible church is never mentioned in the New Testament. He writes, "As for membership in an invisible church without fellowship with any local assembly, this concept is never contemplated in the New Testament. The universal church was the universal fellowship of believers who met visibly in local assemblies.[64]

Why all the debate about the distinction between the universal and local church? Why spend so much time on the etymology of *ekklesia* and its uses in the New Testament? The reason is simple. Misunderstanding the New Testament concept of the church diminishes the importance of the local church to the individual believer. When the local church is trumped by the universal church, personal accountability is minimized, Christian growth is stunted, and practically the local church vanishes. People move from church to church to "bless" each congregation with their "gifts" and insights only to become spiritual pygmies. The work of God in this world is done primarily through the local congregations. That is God's plan.

A story told by Dr. R. G. Lee, the famed pastor of Bellevue Baptist Church in Memphis, TN, illustrates this point. Dr. Lee said a woman who had a beautiful singing voice once wanted to sing in Bellevue's choir. She approached Dr. Lee with the request; he inquired as to her church affiliation. She said that she was a member of the invisible church. He replied, "Fine, then sing in their choir."[65]

The local church is where real accountability should take place. In a local congregation a person is known and builds relationships. If that person falls into sin or grave doctrinal error, the local congregation is to act in great love and hold that person accountable to biblical standards. The church is to act to correct and restore the person.

The church is also described in the New Testament in figurative ways that emphasize differing aspects of her nature. Paul refers to Christians in the church at Corinth as *God's fellow workers, God's field, God's building*.[66] The local church is referenced as the *people of God*,[68] *household of God*,[68] *household of faith*,[69] *bride of Christ*,[70] and *body of Christ*.[71] These metaphors describe a local, particular assembly. To apply these metaphors to the universal church distorts the New Testament meaning.

When Paul writes referring to the church as the *bride of Christ*, the analogy finds its meaning in the marriage of one man and one woman.[72] When a couple stand at the altar of God to take their marriage vows, this man and woman are pledging to be faithful to each other. The man is not promising to love all women but only one. The woman vows to love only one man. Paul says he is speaking of Christ and the church and he illustrates this metaphor using the marriage relationship.

Another metaphor of the church is the body of Christ.[73] Paul talks about the unity between the Head, Christ, and the members, His body. He speaks of the interdependence among the members that make up the body. Christ is the Head who is working His will through the body. Applying this figure of speech to the universal church would be total chaos.

In the universal church application, Christ would be the Head and all the believers in the world would be the body. How would the body function? No coordination between parts of the body would exist. If the analogy were changed to make the members of the body the different churches of all Christian denominations, major problems would still be there. That would mean that one church would be a finger on a hand, while another church might be a toe on the foot. It sounds good, but that would make every member of that "finger" church to have the same gifts. Experience says that is not true.

When the metaphor is applied to a local congregation, the truth becomes clear. Christ is the Head of the local church; every member of that local church makes up the body. Everyone in the local church has differing gifts; they all work together to make the body function. When one member suffers, the whole body (local congregation) suffers. In reality all members of that body need each other; thus the metaphor is illustrated.

The church also has a divine design which is *the pillar and ground of the truth.*[74] The ground or foundation stabilizes the building. A pillar not only is to hold the roof firm but to thrust it high so it can be seen from a distance. The truth and the church have a relationship that is inseparable.

The church rests on the truth. She depends on it and in reality cannot exist without it. The church is called to serve the truth—to hold fast to the truth and to make it known. To dismantle truth would be to tear apart the church. Without truth the church would have no foundation. Truth, however, needs the church for its defense.

Voices in this post-modern society declare that ultimate truth cannot be known—that truth is relative and people cannot know anything for certain. Truths once held concerning doctrine and morals have been dismissed by many believing they are now untruth. Who is speaking out against such foolishness? It certainly is not the intellectual centers of academia, for they are producing such nonsense. It is not liberal evangelicalism, for they are complicit with academia. Only the Bible-believing churches are holding up truth and proclaiming it without apology.

In the old town of Santa Fe, NM, is a picturesque building called the Loretta Chapel. Built hundreds of years ago by the sacrificial efforts of some very determined Catholic nuns, it is famous today for a unique spiral staircase that leads from the sanctuary up to the choir loft.

When the building was under construction and almost finished, the sisters realized the choir had no way to get to its choir loft. They started praying for God to solve this problem. Not long after that a stranger arrived at the mission. In a few days the mysterious carpenter had built the staircase and disappeared.

Today the chapel still stands—not as a mission but as a museum. Many people visit and admire its beauty. But the question arises, "What would the nuns who sacrificed so much for it to be built think about the fact that it is merely a museum?"[75] When a congregation does not stand for the unchanging truth of God, she loses her way and abandons her purpose in the world. Eventually she will become nothing more than a relic of the past.

Chapter 5

Church Membership

Then those who gladly received his word were baptized; and that day about three thousand souls were added to them. And they continued steadfastly in the apostles' doctrine and fellowship, in the breaking of bread, and in prayers (Acts 2:41-42).

Many church leaders today are doing their best to make American Christianity palpable or trendy. They are embarrassed by biblical dogma, mortified by personal evangelism, and made uncomfortable by preaching. They have this great desire to recast Christianity to make it acceptable to the masses. To make the Christian faith reflect the views of post-modern culture, Jesus would be acceptable, even Christianity in general terms may be appropriate, but denominations in particular are definitely not acceptable. Being on mission to help the hungry is great. Being "spiritual" is "in", but the church—well, that is definitely out. Some have even advocated that they are saving their faith by abandoning the church!

Many question the need for the church in the age in which we live. We have television, computers with high-speed Internet and the world-wide web, digital audio and video players, and a vast array of spiritual material—including worship music and videos—to download. The church, some believe, just isn't needed today as it once was before the modern age.

Is such thinking true? Is the church simply some arcane

institution society has outgrown? Without a doubt the church has fallen on tough times. Some of the negative perceptions by society are the fault of the church herself. Stories of sexual abuse by a few ministers and avarice and greed by others have tarnished the testimony of the church. No excuse exists for such abuses, but those infractions do not represent the majority.

The church is here to stay—that is until Jesus comes. Her perpetuity is secure.[76] Jesus *loved the church and gave Himself for her.*[77] The follower of Christ should love the church as well and not abandon her when she gathers for worship.[78] The local church is central to the believer's discipleship and evangelism. Accountability to each other and Christian fellowship are also important ingredients provided only by the congregation.

The questions are then raised, "Is church membership important? Is joining a local church really necessary? Is it even biblical?" Many people are under the impression that joining a church is more traditional than biblical. Other questions surface, "If a person were to join a church, which one would he choose since there are so many? Don't most churches and denominations believe the same things anyway?"

Most mainline denominations subscribe to the historic Christian creeds or have their own confessions of faith.[79] The doctrine delineated by these denominations is similar in many ways; all consider themselves orthodox regardless of how liberal they are. The difference between these denominations is found more in their application of doctrine than in their affirmation of it. Consider this historical illustration.

The reformers that drove the Protestant Reformation were guided by certain biblical principles that became known as the "five *solas.*" These were Latin phrases that summarized the core theology of the reformers against the teachings of the Roman Catholic Church. These principles were *sola scriptura*

(Scripture alone), *sola gratia* (grace alone), *sola fide* (faith alone), *solus Christus* (Christ alone), and *soli Deo gloria* (glory to God alone). The Magisterial Reformers were brave individuals who stood against the power and influence of the Roman Catholic Church to reclaim biblical orthodoxy. The theological reforms were significant to transform churches throughout Europe but still did not go far enough in application of church practice.

A group arose that agreed with the "five *solas*". They believed the Reformation needed not only to purify theology but also the practice of the church. This movement is referred to as the *Radical Reformation*. They rejected infant baptism because they believed that baptism was only for those who had believed in Jesus Christ and demonstrated this by adult baptism. This is called *believer's baptism*. They also believed that the church should not be allied with the government and should not be supported by the state. A complete separation of church and state should exist.

The Magisterial Reformers had their doctrine correct, but their application was misguided. They had embraced the state church as the Roman Catholic Church before wanting to replace the elite in the Roman Catholic Church with their own educational elite. Synonymous with citizenship was church membership primarily through the sprinkling of infants.

The Radical Reformers saw this practice inconsistent with biblical teaching. If salvation was through faith alone, in Christ alone, by grace alone, then the church should consist only of believers. These believers, then, were to demonstrate their faith by baptism. The rediscovery of this New Testament pattern of believers-only baptism and a believers' church began to reformat the doctrine of the church. This was simply a matter of reformational theology being rightly practiced.

All churches are not the same. They may profess right doctrine, such as the Magisterial Reformers did, but not follow through scriptural teaching into the right practice. Both doctrine and practice should be taken into account when considering which church to attend. The question still lingers, "Why join a local church?" The answer is simple. Church membership has a biblical basis.

Believers have a responsibility to each other. They are not to be isolated from each other but to look out for one another. This responsibility is the basis for church membership. The *one-another* commands in Scripture teach this. These commands can be understood only in the context of the local church. *Bear one another's burdens,*[80] *exhort* (encourage) *one another daily,*[81] *the members should have the same care for one another,*[82] are just a few examples of scriptural directives revealing our responsibilities to each other.

These commands tell us how our lives are tied to the lives of others. We are to live in harmony with each other and to care for each other. The Bible reveals that the Christians in the first century had a responsibility to care for the needs of others in their congregation.[83] Christians had no government programs to rely on. They had to rely on each other. "To become a Christian was already to begin one's lifelong journey in the company of pilgrims under the care of the church. Discipleship was defined by churchmanship. Personal faith in Christ was never set over against active membership in the visible body of Christ."[84]

Church membership is necessary for biblical accountability. A distinction is made between responsibility and accountability. If a believer had more than enough goods and another believer was greatly lacking, the one with plenty had a responsibility to share with the brother in need. If he did not discharge his Christian responsibility to share, then he was held accountable to others in the church.

Christians are also to live with spiritual integrity in this world and not to bring reproach to the name of Christ. Should a believer fall into sin and tarnish his testimony, giving cause for others to ridicule the faith, the erring brother should be exhorted to repent. If he does not repent but continues in his wayward course, then the church is to take appropriate action. The Bible gives guidelines for church discipline when necessary. These instructions, however, do not make sense except in the context of membership. Consider what Jesus said: *"Moreover if your brother sins against you, go and tell him his fault between you and him alone. If he hears you, you have gained your brother. But if he will not hear, take with you one or two more, that 'by the mouth of two or three witnesses every word may be established.' And if he refuses to hear them, tell it to the church. But if he refuses even to hear the church, let him be to you like a heathen and a tax collector."*[85] No formal discipline of an erring, unrepentant brother can occur if that brother is simply in an informal relationship with the local church. An organization has no authority over its non-members.

The church at Corinth had many problems. Sexual immorality was reported about a particular member; this astonished the Apostle Paul. He took strong action against this person and chastised the church for her neglect of the situation. Then addressing the church he wrote, *But now I have written to you not to keep company with anyone named a brother, who is sexually immoral, or covetous, or an idolater, or a reviler, or a drunkard, or an extortioner—not even to eat with such a person. For what have I to do with judging those also who are outside? Do you not judge those who are inside? But those who are outside God judges. Therefore "put away from yourselves the evil person."* [86] The believers at Corinth knew who was formally a part of their church and who was not. They knew who was "inside" and who was "outside" the church. They had authority over those "inside" to correct if necessary and had no authority over those "outside." How could they know who was formally "in" and "out" without a voluntary commitment on the part of the individual to become part of their congregation?

Church membership is visible and tangible. After Peter's sermon at Pentecost, Luke records, *Then those who gladly received his word were baptized; and that day about three thousand souls were added to them.*[87] Those added to the congregation by baptism were visible for others to see. Christian baptism identified them with the local congregation. The same is true today. Through baptism people become members of a local church.

When Ananias and Sapphira lied to God and to Peter about some land they sold, they both dropped dead.[88] The result of that incident caused great fear to come on the church and all who heard about it. Although the church was respected, people did not want to *join* because of the mighty acts of God.[89] The word *join*[90] is from the word *glue* meaning to "cleave" or "fasten together." This word is also used in being *joined* in a sexual relationship.[91] The word speaks of a strong bonding relationship in which a voluntary choice is made of joining oneself to another. In this context it refers to those "joining" the local church or rather not wanting to become a part of the group.

Formal church membership also enables pastoral oversight to have clear direction. Pastoral oversight is valid only with the context of a visible, known membership. Paul writes to his son in the ministry, Timothy, *If a man desires the position of a bishop, he desires a good work.*[92] Paul refers to the pastor of a congregation and addresses his responsibilities. What does the pastor oversee? How can he provide oversight if he does not know exactly for whom he is responsible?

In the discharge of the pastor's duties Paul raises the question, *If a man does not know how to rule his own house, how will he take care of the church of God?*[93] Paul compares leading a church with leading a family. The analogy seems obvious. Everyone knows who is in his family. The same should be true in the local church. The members know each other. That is only possible when the people have a formal membership role.

Another biblical rational for church membership is the various metaphors the Bible uses to describe the church. These metaphors will make sense only when they are applied to the local congregation. Some of the analogies were illustrated in the previous chapter when making the distinction between the local church and the church universal. The metaphors have meaning only within the context of church membership in a local church.

The local New Testament church is to be the cutting edge of God's work in this world. Many reject the local church today by stating their animosity against "organized" religion. What do they prefer? "Unorganized" religion? When a person does not join with a local church and become accountable to that congregation, unorganized religion is exactly what is left. God is a God of order and not confusion. Rebellion of the heart is generally the reason the local church is rejected. However, when a person is truly transformed by God's grace, the desire of his or her heart is to link up with a congregation and grow spiritually. This may not be trendy, but it is very biblical.

Chapter 6

Christian Baptism

Therefore we were buried with Him through baptism into
death, that just as Christ was raised from the dead by the
glory of the Father, even so we also should walk
in newness of life
(Rom. 6:40).

The teaching on ecclesiology, the doctrine of the church,
has been practically abandoned by the American evangelical
community for almost a generation. Robert Patterson observed
this reality and wrote:

"Among American evangelicals the doctrine of the church
has practically been abandoned. The almost exclusive emphasis on individual Christian experience and the concomitant
neglect of the corporate life of the people of God is stunting
spiritual growth. Since evangelicals consider themselves the
guardians of orthodoxy, it is strange that they would allow this
weakening of the doctrine of the church, but it is clearly mani-
fested in three areas.

"(1) In addition to the well-documented decline in denominational loyalty, evangelicalism today is characterized by
increasing numbers of Christians who will not commit themselves to a local congregation. (2) Many churches no longer
require baptism as a prerequisite for church membership or
participation in communion. Baptism has become merely an
option, more a celebration of an individual's faith than of

God's grace in joining that person to the body of Christ. (3) Evangelical indifference toward the church is also revealed in their support of parachurch organizations. The real leaders in the evangelical subculture are not denominational heads or ministers but the self-appointed directors of parachurch ministries."[94]

With keen observation, Patterson points out the relationship of the decline of denominational loyalty, unscriptural views of baptism, and indifference toward the church are factors that stunt personal spiritual growth. The church abandoning the importance of baptism and viewing it as an "option" would sound strange to church leaders a generation ago. Yet today churches are acquiescing in their historic position on baptism to the individual's own interpretation of the rite.[95] Is baptism really a biblical option? Some would contend that one baptism is just as good as another because it is a symbolic statement anyway. Is that true? Does the Bible speak clearly on this subject?

In this age of religious pluralism, imagining why people in the 16th century would be tortured or drowned over the issue concerning the mode of baptism is difficult. The Magisterial Reformers during the Reformation were moving away from the Roman Catholic Church doctrinally. The supremacy of Holy Scripture once again was elevated to its rightful place and the biblical doctrine of salvation in Christ alone, by grace alone, through faith alone was rediscovered. These doctrines began to take hold in the churches and changed the face of Christianity throughout Europe.

The Achilles' heel of the Magisterial Reformers was their doctrine of the church, which also impacted their view of church and state. Like the Roman Catholic Church, these Reformers connected the visible church to society as a whole. Their theological reform movement was supported by the government magistrates. Whoever ruled, whether Catholic or

Protestant, used the power of the government to mandate conformity to their theology. Both Catholic and Protestant leaders agreed with infant baptism, because to be a citizen of the state was to be part of the church as well. They viewed baptism not only as a religious issue but a civil issue as well. Baptism then helped to create a seamless Christian society. Whoever disagreed with this view was seen as a transgressor receiving the condemnation from the Church using the power of the State. Therefore, those in the Radical Reformation, which included the Anabaptists, were persecuted by both Catholics and Protestants.

The leaders in the Radical Reformation went deeper in reform and put into practice the theology of the Reformation and rediscovered a believer's church. Where the Reformers wanted to reform the Roman Catholic Church, the Radical Reformers wanted to actually restore the church to her initial purity and practice. This is what led them to the position that baptism had to be understood and applied biblically—thus a believers'-only church.

The serious Christian today will not view baptism as an option. The local church will have an important part in the life of the believer because the church will be viewed as central to Christian growth and discipleship. Determining what the Bible teaches about baptism therefore is important. Volumes have been written about this subject, but the purpose here is to bring a concise view of scriptural teaching.

A biblical baptism must begin with the proper subject, that is, a believer. Repentance from sin and faith in Christ are the necessary graces in the heart of each believer. Sermons preached in the New Testament declared the hearers to repent before they would be baptized.[96] The description Paul used of a believer is one who has died to sin. This death to sin is to occur before we identify in Christ's death through baptism.[97]

New Testament baptism is reserved only for those individuals who have first trusted Christ. The pattern witnessed throughout the New Testament is to believe first and then be baptized. It is never found in reverse order.

A man named Philip was preaching in Samaria to people deceived by a sorcerer named Simon. The Bible says, *But when they believed Philip as he preached the things concerning the kingdom of God and the name of Jesus Christ, both men and women were baptized. Then Simon himself also believed; and when he was baptized he continued with Philip.*[98] The people first believed and then they were baptized.

On another occasion Philip preached to an Ethiopian eunuch returning home from Jerusalem. When Philip was finished telling the man about Christ, the eunuch saw water and asked what would hinder him from being baptized. Philip's response was, *"If you believe with all your heart, you may." And he answered and said, "I believe that Jesus Christ is the Son of God." So he commanded the chariot to stand still. And both Philip and the eunuch went down into the water, and he baptized him.*[99]

After Saul of Tarsus was converted to Christ on the Damascus Road, he was baptized by Ananias.[100] After he preached to them at Cornelius' house, Peter baptized those who trusted in Christ.[101] Paul baptized those who trusted in Christ after the earthquake in the Philippian jail.[102] When Paul was in Corinth sharing the Gospel *Crispus, the ruler of the synagogue, believed on the Lord with all his household. And many of the Corinthians, hearing, believed and were baptized.*[103] In every case the pattern is the same. The people heard the Gospel of Christ preached, they believed the Gospel and surrendered their lives personally to Christ, and then they were baptized.

The only candidate the Bible describes for baptism is a believer. Scripture makes no reference to baptizing anyone other than a believer in Christ. This commitment to Christ must be made personally. It cannot be made in proxy for someone else. A person cannot believe for someone else, nor can a person be baptized for someone else. We also see no New Testament example of baptizing an infant. Since the prerequisite for baptism is a volitional act of belief by an individual, an infant would not be a proper candidate. The decision to baptize an infant is made by a parent or guardian of the child and not the child itself.

Those who support infant baptism refer to Paul's incident in the Philippian jail when he said, *"Believe on the Lord Jesus Christ, and you will be saved, you and your household." Then they spoke the word of the Lord to him and to all who were in his house. And he took them the same hour of the night and washed their stripes. And immediately he and all his family were baptized.*[104] They interpret *household* to include infants and small children. This is an argument from silence. The text however, indicates the Gospel was also preached to everyone in the house. Those in the household that believed would be candidates for baptism.

Scholars also disagree on when infant baptism began. Those interpreting the text previously mentioned advocate for a first-century practice. Others believe infant baptism to be a later practice in the church. By the fourth century infant baptism certainly was widely practiced in the churches.

A biblical baptism should also parallel its biblical meaning, which is symbolic. Baptism is a symbol of salvation. As a symbol it points to something very real and tangible: the death, burial, and resurrection of Jesus Christ. Paul acknowledged this truth when he wrote, *Therefore we were buried with Him* (Christ) *through baptism into death, that just as Christ was raised from the dead by the glory of the Father, even so we also should walk in newness of life.*[105] Baptism represents symbolically what has transpired in the new believer's life spiritually.

Believer's baptism can be likened to a three-act play. Act one is death. Act two is burial. Act three is resurrection. Act one, the person has died to his sin. Now that dead person needs to be buried. Act two, the person is buried in a water grave. Act three, the person arises out of the water; this represents someone coming up out of the grave. Thus baptism is the outward symbolic expression of an inward spiritual experience.

Baptism also points to the work of Christ in salvation. The death, burial, and resurrection of Christ are portrayed in the actions of baptism. The believer in baptism is signifying spiritually his identification with Christ. *For if we have been united together in the likeness of His death, certainly we also shall be in the likeness of His resurrection.*[106]

Baptism being a symbol of salvation is not essential to salvation, though it is an important act of obedience to Christ. The baptismal candidate first must have repented and believed in Christ. Scripturally the person is fully saved on the act of repentance and faith. Baptism can add nothing to that salvation. New Testament salvation is faith in Christ plus nothing. Baptism then does not complete salvation. It cannot save, for salvation is only through Jesus Christ.

Peter preaching at Pentecost told the crowd to "*Repent, and let every one of you be baptized in the name of Jesus Christ for the remission of sins.*"[107] The phrase *for the remission of sins* has led some to in error believe the act of baptism, not the blood of Christ, washes away sin. This understanding is contrary to the whole of the New Testament teaching of salvation. The word *for*[108] refers to result. The people were to be baptized because their sins were remitted when they repented. A similar use is made by Jesus when he said, *"The men of Nineveh will rise up in the judgment with this generation and condemn it, because they repented at the preaching of Jonah."*[109] These people repented because of the preaching of Jonah. A person is baptized because his sins have already been forgiven.

To be biblical, baptism is to be performed in the New Testament way. Every baptism in the New Testament was by immersion. The biblical writers know nothing of sprinkling in relation to Christian baptism. The Bible teaches that the believer died with Christ and is buried with Christ. The only kind of baptism that symbolizes burial would be immersion. In any other form the symbol would be meaningless.

The Greek word *baptizo* is what has been transliterated in the English Bibles as *baptize.* When literally translated it means "to immerse or submerge"[110] When the New Testament speaks of baptizing a believer, it always uses this word. A form of the word "sprinkle," is also found in the New Testament. It is from the Greek word *rhantizo?* and is used only three times in the New Testament, all of them in the book of Hebrews. None of the references is used in connection with Christian baptism.

Another word that some may relate to this issue is the word wash. It is the Greek word *louo*; it is used six times in the New Testament. It is used primarily to bathe or wash one's body. Again, none are used with baptism.

From a linguistic standpoint, the language of the New Testament is clear when understanding baptism in biblical times is concerned. The biblical way is immersion. In fact, founders of present-day, mainline denominations have also testified to that truth. Martin Luther, founder of the Lutheran denomination, testified, "I would have the candidates for baptism completely immersed in the water, as the word says, and as the sacrament signifies."[111] John Calvin, founder of the Presbyterian denomination, agreed, "the term *baptizo* means to immerse, and that this was the form used by the primitive Church."[112] John Wesley, founder of the Methodist denomination, affirmed, "We are buried with him, alluding to the ancient manner of baptizing by immersion."[113] Even the Roman Catholic James Cardinal Gibbons said, "For several centuries after the establishment of Christianity, baptism was usually conferred by immersion, but since the 12th century the practice of baptizing by affusion has prevailed in the Catholic Church, as this manner is attended with less inconvenience than baptism by immersion."[114]

A final component of biblical baptism is the authority by which it is administered. Evangelicals have division among them on this issue. Non-evangelicals are unified in believing that baptism resides under church authority and is to be administered by an officer of the church.

The question debated among evangelicals is whether the authority to baptize is individual or congregational. Is baptism an individual Christian ordinance? Can any Christian without any connection or direction from a local church baptize whomever they deem acceptable? Or is baptism a local-church ordinance to be administered by a believer under the authority and direction of the local church?

Those that advocate baptism to be an individual Christian ordinance believe that Jesus gave the Great Commission[115] to individual believers. They affirm that the directives in the Commission to "go, preach, baptize and teach" are to be done by every believer under the mandate of Christ. This position also points to Philip baptizing the Ethiopian eunuch[116] without any outside authority other than the believing Ethiopian needed to be baptized.

The fact believers are called to be witnesses and share the Gospel with others is true. God does call others to teach and preach. The question is whether any believer can indiscriminately baptize on his own. A corollary question would be whether a believer is really to teach and preach apart from a local church also.

The Bible teaches that in the church believers are accountable to each other. Someone not connected to the local church and acting outside her authority has accountability to no one. Consider a person on his own independently preaching. To whom is this person accountable should he preach a wrong Gospel? The same holds true in a teaching position as well.

When a believer baptizes someone independently of the local church, to whom is the person accountable? If any baptized believer can baptize another person apart from the local church, what would hinder a 10-year-old from baptizing an 8-year-old? Or vice versa? The end result would be chaotic, with many lone-ranger Christians running around.

The Great Commission was given by Jesus to the church. The disciples gathered together in one locale to receive the Commission would constitute a church. In Matthew's gospel the commission was given to *the eleven disciples*,[117] in Mark's gospel it was given to *the eleven*,[118] in Luke's gospel it was given to *the eleven and those who were with them*,[119] in John's gospel the commission was given to *the disciples*.[120]

The Apostle Paul understood the Great Commission to be given to the local church. Paul, while addressing a local congregation, stated the commission in corporate terms. To the congregation in Colosse Paul says *Him we preach, warning every man and teaching every man.*[121] Paul wrote in his second letter to the church in Corinth, *Now then, we are ambassadors for Christ, as though God were pleading through us: we implore you on Christ's behalf, be reconciled to God.*[122]

When a pastor preaches to a local congregation and exhorts the people to witness, the people take that exhortation personally and witness individually. Yet it is all done under the auspices of the local church. The directives within the Great Commission were to the church, including baptism. Baptism is a church ordinance.

Parachurch organizations such as Campus Crusade for Christ or the Billy Graham Evangelistic Association even recognize that baptism is a church ordinance. When someone in a Billy Graham Crusade surrenders to Christ, that person is directed to a local church for baptism. Billy Graham's organization does not baptize anyone.

Baptism is performed under the authority of the local church and is a prerequisite to membership in the local church. Baptism reveals that "the believer gives himself to God as he gives to the people of God to walk with them in church relation. The duties connected with church membership are included among the commands which are referred to in the great commission and which are taught after baptism."[123]

The Great Commission is the church's mandate and is her outline for missions and ministry. The place which baptism holds in the commission indicates its use. The church is to make disciples and teach them all the things Jesus commanded. However, an intermediate act—baptism—is required.

A small country church was having a "baptizing" in a river on a cold January day. A revival meeting had just concluded. The preacher asked one of the baptismal candidates, "Is the water cold?" "Naw," he replied. One of the deacons shouted, "Dip him ag'in, preacher; he's still lyin.'" Baptism is that outward symbol of the inward spiritual experience of God's grace in salvation.

Chapter 7

The Purpose of the Church

*And Jesus came and spoke to them, saying,
"All authority has been given to Me in heaven and on earth.
Go therefore and make disciples of all the nations, baptizing
them in the name of the Father and of the Son and of the Holy
Spirit, teaching them to observe all things that I have
commanded you; and lo, I am with you always,
even to the end of the age. Amen*
(Matt. 28:18-20).

In the *Peanuts* comic strip written by Charles Shultz, a ter-
rible breakdown of responsibility occurred somewhere. Lucy
asks Charlie Brown, "Why do you think we're put here on
earth, Charlie Brown?"

"To make others happy," he replies. Pausing, he says,"I
don't think I'm making anyone very happy."

"Of course," she adds, "nobody's making me very happy
either." Then, shouting so loud that she causes Charlie Brown
to do a flip, Lucy yells, "Somebody's not doing his job."

Looking at the condition of Christianity in America, a
breakdown somewhere seems apparent. Someone is slacking
in the discharge of duties. Churches are losing their effectiveness; the number of people attending church regularly is
declining. Noting this decline, church leaders from all denominations have addressed the situation and have called for action.
In the past several decades an intentional effort to reinvigorate
declining churches and reverse this downward spiral has

occurred. New ideas and creative ways to do "church" have been proposed and marketed through conferences and "church-growth networks." We find the transitional church, the seeker-sensitive church, market-driven church, post-modern church, ancient-future church, simple church, purpose-driven church, emergent church, biker church, and cowboy church.

Churches are exploring creative and novel ways to attract the unchurched. They seem to be more interested in pleasing people than in pleasing God. Pragmatism rules the day as long as it can be justified in some moral way. Anything and everything is acceptable as long as it works. This attitude brings to memory a sign at a dude ranch. The sign read "We aim to please at this ranch. For big people we have big horses, for little people we have little horses, for people who want to ride fast we have fast horses, for people who want to ride slow we have slow horses, and for people who have never ridden a horse we have horses that have never been ridden."

Could the problem of declining churches be occurring because churches desire more to conform to culture than to be counter-cultural? A whole host of books (including this one) and articles have been written to help churches get back on track. They all have differing views of what is the main task of the church. Some will advance that the main task of the church is worship, while others will declare it is to meet the felt needs of people. Still others will say the main task is evangelism. The more socially minded believe the main task of the church is to feed the hungry and take care of the underprivileged and poor in our society. Some think the church's task is to advance social justice.

These various views have merit, but do they hit the target? The church should probably contain some of the aspects mentioned, but what about her primary purpose? What would be considered the central focus of the church? Churches do a lot of good things, but do they do the best thing? What is the church to do that no other organization can do?

The last words of a dying person are considered to be extremely important. They are the words by which the person generally will be remembered. They are true words of the heart. The last words of Jesus to His followers are found in the Great Commission. This was the mandate from the Master. The mandate sounds simple but is profound. *"Make disciples of all the nations."*[124]

To whom this command was addressed is a divided question. Was Jesus speaking to individual believers or to the local church? At first glance Jesus would appear to be addressing individuals but a closer examination reveals His command was to the early, primitive church. The Gospels' references of the early church primarily were to the disciples gathered together. Others could have been gathered with them, but the first church basically was identified with the disciples. You had identifiable people (the disciples) gathered together in an identifiable place (the mountain) at an appointed time. Those ingredients make up a New Testament church (*ekklesia*). This book's chapter on Christian baptism more fully discusses this issue.

Some would argue that the church did not begin until Pentecost. Jesus, however, started building His church during His earthly ministry. In Caesarea Philippi Jesus asked the disciples what others are saying about Him. Peter's insightful reply led Jesus to say, *"And I also say to you that you are Peter, and on this rock I will build My church, and the gates of Hades shall not prevail against it."*[125] We find many interpretations of this passage, but one thing is clear. Jesus said, *"I will build My church."* Jesus began building His church when He called the first disciples. He continues to build His church today.

Jesus Christ is the *foundation*[126] and *chief cornerstone*[127] of the church. Naturally these verses are metaphorical in nature, yet that does not diminish the fact that Jesus began the church's construction during His ministry on earth. *And God has appointed these in the church: first apostles, second prophets, third teachers, after that miracles, then gifts of healings, helps, administrations, varieties of tongues.*[128] A church had to exist for God to put apostles in it.

Apostle was "the official name of those twelve of the disciples chosen by our Lord to be with Him during His ministry and to whom He entrusted the organization of His church."[129] After Judas Iscariot betrayed Jesus and hung himself, the disciples felt led to replace him. Peter outlined the original qualification of an apostle necessary for Judas' replacement. *Therefore, of these men who have accompanied us all the time that the Lord Jesus went in and out among us, beginning from the baptism of John to that day when He was taken up from us, one of these must become a witness with us of His resurrection.*[130] Matthias was chosen by the casting of lots.

The church began with the ministry of Jesus, not at Pentecost. The significance of Pentecost is the empowering of the church with the public inauguration of the ministry of the Holy Spirit. The Acts of the Apostles is really a chronicle of the Holy Spirit's ministry and work in the early church. Some have even suggested a more accurate title would be "The Acts of the Holy Spirit." Jesus had a public inauguration of His ministry as well. That occurred at His baptism by John the Baptist. Jesus began the church during His ministry. In Acts, the spreading of the church by the Holy Spirit is seen beginning on the day of Pentecost. What Jesus began in the Gospels, He continues in Acts.

All four Gospels end with the concluding theme of a commission. Christ passed His mission to the church with the promise of His presence. The church is to go into the world and finish what Christ began. The power of the risen Christ is available to His disciples. The command of the risen Christ is given to His disciples. The promise of the risen Christ is their comfort. Nothing shall rob them of His presence. Christ has sovereign control when he states, *"All authority has been given to Me in heaven and on earth."*[131]

The Gospels begin with the assurance of God's presence with us. An angel of the Lord appeared to Joseph in a dream that calmed his fears about marrying Mary. This miraculous birth was a fulfillment of a prophecy by Isaiah *"Behold, the virgin shall be with child, and bear a Son, and they shall call His name Immanuel," which is translated, "God with us."*[132] At the beginning of the Gospel is the promise that God is with us. The Gospel concludes with that same promise of His presence as Christ Jesus sends His church out to evangelize the world and make disciples of all nations.

The authority of Christ is also accented in this directive. All power and authority is His. This authority is what enables the church to accomplish the mission He has mandated. Assigning people a task but not giving them the commensurate authority to carry out that task is the cruel action of a weak leader. Jesus Christ has assigned His church the task of world evangelism. He also has given her the commensurate power to fulfill that task. We have no excuses for failure.

The risen Lord has given His church a singular command, *"Go therefore and make disciples of all the nations, baptizing them in the name of the Father and of the Son and of the Holy Spirit, teaching them to observe all things that I have commanded you."*[133] This singular command expresses the desired purpose of Christ for His church. The command contains only one verb—*make disciples*—which is the singular command. The *"go"* in the command is a participle and should more accurately read *"going,"* or *"while you are going."* *"Baptizing"* and *"teaching"* are also participles, which are verbal adjectives dependent on the main verb *"make disciples."*

Christ's purpose for the church is found in the singular command of the Great Commission—*make disciples.* Disciple-making is a three-fold process described in the three participles. The process begins with going. The idea is not something like a preplanned vacation that begins and ends on a certain date. The idea is more of a lifestyle—the patterns and habits in living your everyday life.

A Christian witness is not something someone "does" as much as it is something someone "is." The action of doing is the result of being. Yes, believers will, from time to time, go to a certain place to meet an individual in order to share the Gospel with him or her. However, the idea is more of a regular lifestyle than a distinct event.

Wherever believers are going, they are to share the Gospel. Biblical Christians are mission-minded people. They are evangelistic. Before a person becomes a disciple, someone must go and tell that person about Jesus. Paul, the Apostle, delineates this process logically to the church in Rome when he says, *For "whoever calls on the name of the Lord shall be saved." How then shall they call on Him in whom they have not believed? And how shall they believe in Him of whom they have not heard? And how shall they hear without a preacher? And how shall they preach unless they are sent?*[134] The end result of making disciples first begins with the going.

The application of the Great Commission is actually a Baptist distinctive in which the Baptist forefathers suffered greatly. The Magisterial Reformers (Luther, Calvin, Melanchthon, Zwingli, etc.) had no missionary vision or missionary spirit. They believed the Great Commission had expired at the end of the Apostolic age. The Anabaptists, however, believed the Great Commission to be binding on every church member in all times. These Radical Reformers looked on the whole world as missionary territory. They believed that this missionary command was most faithfully obeyed in the early church; they wanted to recover that lost virtue. The Anabaptists believed their faith rested on nothing but the commands of Christ. They took seriously the sequence in the Great Commission—the Gospel first, then faith followed, and then baptism followed faith. The order must be maintained for true Christianity to be biblical.

The Magisterial Reformers resisted the "wandering" of the Anabaptists in their missionary enterprise. The Reformers were irritated by the missionary zeal of the Anabaptists and derided them as "spiritual gypsies" and "enthusiasts." Justus Menius, the famous Lutheran polemicist against the Anabaptists, stated bluntly, "God sent only the apostles into all the world."[135] Menius disdained the missionary zeal of the Anabaptists and responded to their charge that the Reformers did not practice what they preached. Endeavoring to justify himself and his fellow reformers because they did not "go into all the world," Menius wrote, "we don't wander around in the world like the Apostles, but stay put and have definite residence and also have our appointed pay."[136]

The New Testament pattern of evangelism is: out into the world and then bringing the converts into the church confessing Christ in their baptism. The Bible is clear that believers are to go out into the world. Nowhere does Scripture say the unchurched are to go to the church. Christians are to go out and win them.

The idea of believers taking the Gospel to all the world is basically neglected today. Yes, world evangelism is emphasized, but what about neighborhood and community evangelism? Too many church members today do not see evangelism as their responsibility but rather that of the pastor. Many congregations pay the pastor to preach, win the lost, and build the believers. The members simply function as spectators or cheerleaders. This is far from the New Testament pattern.

Many people simply believe that because they attend worship on Sunday, they are serving the Lord. No. They are to be out in the world making disciples. Worship is designed to exalt the Lord and give Him praise due His Name. In worship the believer is touched by God, spiritually renewed, and thrust out into the world to serve.

The process of making disciples continues with baptizing. First going, then baptizing. Baptizing presupposes the person has already believed in Christ. As seen in earlier chapters, the New Testament pattern is to believe first and then be baptized. Biblical baptism is by immersion only on the individual's profession of faith in Christ into a local church. An earlier chapter has discussed this.

Jesus spelled out how this would take place—*"baptizing them in the name of the Father and of the Son and of the Holy Spirit."*[137] The triune God was involved in the baptism of Jesus by John the Baptist. *And immediately, coming up from the water, He saw the heavens parting and the Spirit descending upon Him like a dove. Then a voice came from heaven, "You are My beloved Son, in whom I am well pleased."*[138] The triune God is also involved in Christian baptism.

The final process in making disciples is *"teaching them to observe all things I* (Jesus) *have commanded you."*[139] How does a person know what Christ has commanded? The commands and teachings of Christ are found in the Bible, God's Word. *All Scripture is given by inspiration of God, and is profitable for doctrine, for reproof, for correction, for instruction in righteousness, that the man of God may be complete, thoroughly equipped for every good work.*[140]

76

The Bible is our final authority for matters of faith and practice. It is a priceless treasure of divine truth. To learn about God and how to order one's life, look no further than the Bible. When Jesus was in the wilderness being tempted by the devil, he said, *"It is written, 'Man shall not live by bread alone, but by every word of God.'"*[141] A disciple is a learner and should feast on God's Word. The whole counsel of God is to be taught by the church to the disciples. When Paul was in Ephesus before he went to Jerusalem, he stated, *For I have not shunned to declare to you the whole counsel of God.*[142]

Making disciples is the command of Jesus and the purpose of the church. This process will be ongoing until Jesus returns. It is a rigorous one that cannot be altered without violating biblical authority. The future of the church depends on the obedience to the commission.

Perhaps when Jesus ascended to heaven after His mission on earth, the angels asked Him, "Did you accomplish your task?" "Yes, all is finished," the Lord replied. "We have a second question," said the angels. "Has the whole world heard of you?" "No," answered Jesus. The angels next asked, "Then what is your plan?" Jesus said, "I have left 12 men and some other followers to carry the message to the whole world." The angels looked at him and asked, "What is your Plan B?" He replied, "I have no Plan B."

SECTION THREE: LOOKING FORWARD

Chapter 8

Athenian Babel

*And they took him and brought him to the Areopagus, saying,
"May we know what this new doctrine is of which you speak?
For you are bringing some strange things to our ears.
Therefore we want to know what these things mean." For all
the Athenians and the foreigners who were there spent their
time in nothing else but either to tell or to hear some new thing*
(Acts 17:19-21).

The world's richest uranium deposit was discovered by
geologists for Queensland Mines Ltd in a tiny plot of ground
in Australia's remote northern Nabarlek region. The mining
company assumed the rights could be easily secured from the
aboriginal owners, so the industrialists quickly signed $60 mil-
lion worth of contracts to sell the ore to the Japanese. The
mining executives, however, failed to take into account that
the aboriginal owners of the land would refuse to disturb a
colony of green ants located within 200 yards of the site.

In aboriginal religion this was known as Gabo Djang (the
Dreaming Place of the Green Ants.) They believe if the sacred
ground is desecrated, the green ants will turn into man-eating
monsters who will ravage the world. The feelings of the aborigines were so strong that they refused offers of almost $14
million. Given the choice between poverty and the wrath of
the green ants, the aborigines decided to remain poor.[143]

The religious superstitions between the Australian aborig-

81

ines and the Athenian intellectuals were amazingly similar. The intellectuals on Mars Hill preferred their bankrupt philosophy to the vast wealth of the Gospel message preached by Paul. This situation is not unlike what is found today in the intellectual centers of our country. The intellectual elite snub their noses and deride the Gospel message. We Americans may appear more sophisticated because of wealth and even more knowledgeable because of advanced technology. Yet the verdict of God declares, *"I will destroy the wisdom of the wise, and bring to nothing the understanding of the prudent."*[144] *God has chosen the foolish things of the world to put to shame the wise, and God has chosen the weak things of the world to put to shame the things which are mighty . . . that no flesh should glory in His presence.*[145]

The Apostle Paul was not impressed by the brilliance of these sages nor by the beauty and magnificence of the city. The splendor of Greece in the fifth-century B.C. had faded by the time of Paul, but Athens was still a vital intellectual and cultural center. The buildings and monuments of the city were unrivaled. Even today in partial ruins, the Parthenon is a very impressive sight.

Paul did not enjoy the city because he was distressed to see it taken over by idols. The word translated *given over to idols* carries the idea of "under them." We might say the city was "swamped or smothered with idols."[146] Everywhere Paul looked, he saw an idol. A present day parallel would be the city of Las Vegas, NV. Instead of an "idol", you find a slot machine everywhere you go. The intellectual capital of the world produced idolatry. The art reflected that idolatrous worship and caused Paul to be very uncomfortable.

Insight into how this idolatry affected Paul can be found in the verb *provoked*. This is the verb generally used in the Septuagint (LXX), the Greek translation of the Old Testament

Hebrew, of God's particular reaction to idolatry.[147] God is a jealous God and was provoked to anger at Israel's idolatry. In the same way, the feelings aroused by the Apostle Paul in Athens were the emotions of his abhorrence of the idolatry he witnessed.[148]

Xenophon (431-355 B.C.), the Greek historian, referred to Athens as "one great altar, one great sacrifice."[149] Observers in the city declared, "there were more gods in Athens than in all the rest of the country, and the Roman satirist hardly exaggerates when he says that it was easier to find a god there than a man."[150] The city was consumed by cultured paganism that was fed by idolatry, novelty, and philosophy. Greek philosophy had humanized God and deified man.

Much of what occurred in the ancient city of Athens and in Greek culture in general is what is taking place in the intellectual centers of today. Visit the great universities; you will find elaborately constructed buildings—some even in the architectural genre of ancient Greece. These academic centers seem to be captivated by novelty and intoxicated with philosophy, yet they are just as spiritually and morally bankrupt as Athens in Paul's day.

Some of these world-renowned intellectual centers even house theological schools that have been the seedbeds of abhorrent, unorthodox Christian doctrine and destructive methodology in theology. Some of the theological schools and seminaries were begun by mainline denominations and originally taught orthodox Christian doctrine in the training of their students for Christian ministry. Most of them today have severed the formal ties they once had with their respective denominations and have deserted the orthodox theology once taught.

Universalism, the idea that all people are going to heaven, can readily be found on many of our campuses. The philosophy most espoused is that all religions are good and simply teach different ways of going to heaven or some blissful after-life. Even some of the cults from Scientology to Kaballa to New Age are being taught. All of these are simply reinvented religious philosophy generated from ancient times.

Though the city of Athens depressed Paul because the city was given over to idolatry, he began to dialogue with the people there. He started in the synagogue and in the marketplace discussing Jesus and the resurrection with the curious. Those attending synagogue certainly would know something of the teachings about the Messiah. Even though the Jews in the synagogue would not see Jesus as the Messiah, this was generally the first place Paul went when he traveled to a new city. Evidently this discussion continued from the synagogue out into the marketplace, where he encountered the philosophers of the day.

The dialogue with these philosophers evidently became a little more rigorous as they *encountered* him. This is a more aggressive word used to describe the scene. The word is used of "encountering" in war or debate.[151] Paul may have adopted the Socratic method of dialogue; this method involves questions and answers. This exchange with these philosophers was a little more aggressive. Intellectuals seem to be more contentious against spiritual truth!

These philosophers were identified. One group was the Epicureans and the other the Stoics. The Epicureans were the "philosophers of the gardens" founded by Epicurus (c341-270 B.C.). He considered the gods to be so remote as to have no interest in and no influence on human life. Everything was due by chance. He taught that no life after death and no judgment existed. Truth is to be sought by personal experience and not by reason, because the world happened because of chance. Therefore, the goal is life should be the pursuit of pleasure and fine living. Human beings should pursue pleasure detached from pain, passion, and fear.

The philosophy of Epicurus sounds much like what is being espoused in American contemporary society, even within some religious circles. Those that advocate and embrace a "prosperity gospel" have a lot in common with this philosophy. The pursuit of pleasure and fine living known as the "good life" is a hallmark of the prosperity gospel which seems to have more in common with Epicurean philosophy than biblical theology. Truth, sought by personal experience and not by biblical revelation, can also be heard from some pulpits. Everything seems to be measured by personal experience and feelings.

Charismatic churches are guilty of this, though none would confess to it. Most of their adherents derive their theology from personal experience and then proof-text that experience by the Bible. Their whole Christian experience seems to be based on feelings. They are strong on feelings and short on biblical theology. This can be the only reason why Charismatics would embrace someone like the now-dethroned Charismatic evangelist Todd Bentley.[152] Sadly, Bentley is not the only evangelist in those circles that has been extreme. The movement, more than any other group, has been riddled with various excesses. Why? Any time feelings reign supreme and trump biblical orthodoxy, wild excesses and bad theology will result.

The other philosophical group that Paul encountered in Athens was the Stoics. The name derives from the porch (*stoa* or painted colonnade) next to the Agora where they taught. These were the "philosophers of the porch." This philosophy was founded by Zeno (344-262 B.C.) The stoics rejected pagan worship and acknowledged a supreme god but in a pantheistic way—that is god is the all. This philosophy taught that the world is determined by fate and that we must live in harmony with nature and reason. Chance was out of the equation. Everything, including human decisions and behavior, is determined by an unbroken chain of prior events. The results lead to a prideful life in which no one really needs God's help.

Descendants of this philosophical system are prevalent in contemporary society as well. The extreme environmentalists who do not discern the difference in the intrinsic worth of a spotted owl or human being is an example. The New Age movement with its "oneness of humanity" would be an ancestor as well. Where Epicureanism emphasizes feelings, Stoicism primarily rejects feelings altogether and highlights reason. A stoic is one who is simply indifferent to anything.

The religion of Greece with its attendant philosophies was destitute of moral and spiritual power. It was a religion that accented amusement on one hand and the arts on the other. It also continued to seek something new. These three aspects of this ancient religion can be seen in different aspects of the contemporary religious scene in America.

In liberal Protestant churches intellectualism has replaced the authority of the Bible. The Gospel of Christ is no longer preached; more often than not, it is derided. The arts and their esoteric value have been elevated in their place. High-church music, beautiful stained glass, and museum quality art are central aspects of their churches.

The contemporary Christian movement with its variegated streams is entertaining its followers with various amusements. The pop culture has invaded the church to amuse worshipers with music videos, mimes, dramas, concerts, and a whole host of "creative" worship styles. All are designed to entertain the attendees.

The constant appetite for novelty seems insatiable by this generation. People who are always chasing the new and ignoring the old will soon realize that they have no roots to secure and nourish their lives. Paul was not amused by the novelty he observed in Athens. On the contrary he was very distressed by it. His roots were deep in Christ; he had no need for the offerings in Athens.

The wisest man that ever lived, King Solomon, wrote, *And there is nothing new under the sun*.[153] If it is new, it probably isn't true. If it is true, it probably isn't new. We are not to be mesmerized by the fads and trends of the day. They wax and wane. However, this does not mean the Gospel is not to be contextualized. Paul did not try to be clever and make the Gospel popular to the Athenian culture. The Scriptures declare that Paul preached "Jesus and the resurrection."[154] to these intellectuals.

The word translated *preach* is *euaggelizo*. It means "to bring good news." Every place in the New Testament in which the Gospel is "preached", this word is used. Paul did not try to debate with these people; he simply declared the Gospel. He preached doctrine to them.

Notice the doctrine Paul preached at Athens. He preached the power of God in creation as he declared *"God, who made the world and everything in it."*[155] The great existential questions of our time, "Where did I come from? Why am I here? Where am I going?" are asked by everyone. Science attempts to answer where we came from. Philosophers attempt to answer why we are here. But only the Christian faith has the answer to all three.

The Epicureans were practical atheists who believed that matter is everything and that it is eternal. The Stoics were pantheists and believed that God didn't create anything but organized matter and set it in motion. This is like the Deists of today. However, Paul affirmed creation by declaring that God created everything.

The doctrine Paul preached also told of God's provision. God *"gives to all life, breath, and all things."*[156] God doesn't need us. We need Him. God is self-sufficient and does not need human provisions. God is the One who provides us with life and material needs.

Paul's message also addressed the providence of God. God *"has determined their preappointed times and the boundaries of their dwellings, so that they should seek the Lord."*[157] This declaration would strike a blow to their Athenian pride and would reveal that they had a common ancestry as the rest of the world being *"made from one blood."* They were no better than other people. Paul's statement also underscored the immanence of God. The Greeks believed in the transcendence of God and that He had no concern for man or his needs. Paul is stating and otherwise affirming that God is involved in every person's life.

The Apostle also outlined the plan of God. *"But now commands all men everywhere to repent, because He has appointed a day on which He will judge the world in righteousness."*[158] God has been patient until now but no longer. Since the resurrection of Christ from the dead everyone will give an account of his life to God.

The three areas in which Jesus said the Holy Spirit would convict people[159], we see in Paul's preaching to these philosophers. Paul spoke on the subject of sin and their need to repent and of righteousness and judgment of the world to come.

They could not accept the doctrine of the resurrection. It was nonsense to the Greek mind that a dead person could be raised from the dead and live forever. Many today refuse to accept the resurrection of Christ. Yet a person must embrace this truth if he or she becomes a follower of Christ. Paul wrote to the church at Rome and declared, *That if you confess with your mouth the Lord Jesus and believe in your heart that God has raised Him from the dead, you will be saved. For with the heart one believes unto righteousness, and with the mouth confession is made unto salvation.*[160]

The reaction to Paul's message is the same today by many people. Some mocked, some wanted to hear more, and others believed. Those who mocked Paul probably chided him for being intolerant and having such a narrow worldview. Can you hear those voices today? They might say such things as, "How dare you think you have the truth? You are too closed-minded."

These philosophers derided Paul by referring to him as a "*babbler*", which literally means "seed-picker." Actually, the babbling was done by these Athenian philosophers as they rambled on with each other as they looked for something new. Some finally found the truth for which they had been searching. It was in the person of Jesus Christ.

Chapter 9

Modern Ministry

Preach the word! Be ready in season and out of season.
Convince, rebuke, exhort, with all longsuffering and teaching.
For the time will come when they will not endure sound
doctrine, but according to their own desires, because they
have itching ears, they will heap up for themselves teachers;
and they will turn their ears away from the truth,
and be turned aside to fables
(2 Tim. 4:2-4).

The well-known phrase, "the more things change, the more they stay the same," is highly appropriate in Christian ministry. Today we are hearing a cacophony of voices telling us how the world is changing and that the church must also change. If the church refuses to change, she will become irrelevant. Many suggest the church is already irrelevant.

In 1994 the Barna Research Group asked Americans the following question: "Do you agree or disagree that the churches in your area are relevant to the way you live today?"[161] In response, 65 percent of non-Christians agreed. Possibly more significant was the reply of the "born-again Christians"—85 percent of whom agreed that the Christian Church is relevant for today.

What caused the church to be pronounced *irrelevant* to those surveyed? Could it be the church has lost focus on Jesus Christ and her mission in this world? Has the church abandoned the Gospel and embraced the culture, thus becoming some kind of hybrid that is rejected by both the world and the church? Is this the kind of church Jesus had in mind when He said, *"I know your works, that you are neither cold nor hot. I could wish you were cold or hot. So then, because you are lukewarm, and neither cold nor hot, I will vomit you out of My mouth."*[162] William Willimon confessed, "Sometime in my ministry, the church I served changed from being a church desiring to be salt to a church desiring to be honey to help the world's solutions go down a bit easier. At first I thought it was a problem of liberal vs. conservative, or peacemaking vs. warmaking. But lately I've decided it reflects the more fundamental problem of the church and the world."[163]

There has always been the tension between the church and the world. Jesus and the New Testament writers warned of the church becoming too worldly. *Do not love the world or the things in the world. If anyone loves the world, the love of the Father is not in him. For all that is in the world—the lust of the flesh, the lust of the eyes, and the pride of life—is not of the Father but is of the world,*[164] warns the Apostle John. Ministry in this modern world is confronted with the same heart issues of previous centuries. How can the church stay true to the teachings of Christ and be effective in this world?

The Apostle Paul wrote to Timothy, his young protégée, as he was nearing the end of his life and ministry. He was leaving the responsibility for care of the churches and leadership in maintaining the *faith once delivered to the saints* to him. At this time, Timothy was probably around 40-years old and was under a great deal of strain. He suffered frequent illnesses[165] and faced opposition because of his youthfulness.[166] These two issues, however, were not the greatest challenges of this young man. The greatest challenge he faced was his preaching ministry.

He confronted challenges from two directions. The first was from a world that was going mad. His times and his world were perilous, with families unraveling and society in turmoil.[167] The second challenge was from problems within the church. The church had lost her moorings. People were looking for novelty and turning away from sound teaching.[168]

A battle for truth was being waged within the church. Truth was an important issue to Paul especially in giving pastoral advice to Timothy and Titus.[169] This same "truth battle" is raging in contemporary Christianity today. John MacArthur has aptly noted, "People are experimenting with subjective, relativistic ideas of truth and labeling them 'Christian.' This trend signals a significant departure from biblical and historic Christianity."[170]

King Solomon wrote, "Do not remove the ancient landmark which your fathers have set."[171] Some people today would deconstruct the Christian faith and rebuild it according to their pattern. Those that adhere to absolute truth, as their forefathers did, are chided as not being relevant. The ancient landmark described by King Solomon is under tremendous assault, particularly by those who are called to uphold truth. Vincent of Lerins wrote:

"I cannot help wondering about such madness in certain people, the dreadful impiety of their blinded minds, their insatiable lust for error that they are not content with the traditional rule of faith as once and for all received from antiquity but are driven to seek another novelty daily. They are possessed by a permanent desire to change religion, to add something and to take something away – as though the dogma were not divine so that it has to be revealed only once. But they take it for a merely human institution, which cannot be perfected except by constant emendations, rather, by constant corrections."[172]

How does Paul advise Timothy to address these challenges? Does he tell him to search out the latest idea or try the most recent marketing technique? No, Paul tells Timothy to preach the Word of God without *fear*[173] and teach the people *in humility*.[174] Paul is admonishing Timothy to have a ministry based in Scripture and proclaimed by preaching.

Timothy understood fully what Paul meant when he was told to preach the Word. The word *preach* conveys a picture of the Emperor's spokesman, the Imperial Herald, proclaiming in a formal, authoritative manner a message the Emperor gave him to announce. It also suggests a picture of the town official making a proclamation in a public gathering.

This should be the pattern for the modern-day preacher. He is conscious of the fact that he is an official herald of Jesus Christ. The Word of God should be delivered with the soberness and dignity commensurate with the task. Tragically, however, this is not true in many pulpits today. Biblical preaching has fallen on tough times in the contemporary church.

Alternative church leaders convened an Emergent Church Conference in San Diego in 2005. Some of the presenters said that preaching was broken. They advocate that preaching can take on many forms. They said the old way of preaching is passé. Suggestions included watching film clips and discussing them or discussing lectionary reading talk-show style. Any and all creative ideas could be exchanged for old-time preaching.

This approach is contrary to the advice Paul gave Timothy to preach the Word of God. Why would a church leader dismiss the biblical injunction to preach the Word and substitute some alternative in its place? Is the Word of God sufficient to change lives? Do we really believe the preaching of the cross is the power of God unto salvation? When film clips and talk-show-style settings are substituted for preaching, has faith in the power of the Gospel been lost?

Paul advised Timothy in perilous times to preach the Word

of God even though some will have *itching ears* that want to hear something new. Don't be sidetracked by novelty but to stay the course. *Hold fast the pattern of sound words,*[175] *but you must continue in the things which you have learned,*[176] *be ready in season and out of season,*[177] are some of the admonitions to stay strong. With these admonitions, Paul keeps bringing Timothy back to the unchangeable Word of God.[178] The Holy Scriptures were to be the anchor of his life and foundation for his ministry.

From his childhood Timothy had learned the Scriptures; they pointed him to salvation in Christ. Now Paul was reminding him of the critical role the Scriptures were to play in his present ministry. Paul underscores the origin of the Scriptures as being from God and not man. They are by the inspiration of God[179] and are without error. Paul asserts the primacy of the Scriptures in all aspects of Timothy's ministry.

The Scriptures are to be used as the basis for teaching others God's truth. Some in the church strayed from sound teaching because of *itching ears.*"They were abandoning the authority of the Bible in their teaching and seeking after new ideas. As Paul tells Timothy, teaching biblical doctrine is foundation for Christian growth.

The Scriptures also are beneficial for reproof. This is the only place in the New Testament this word *reproof* is used. It is translated from *elegmos* and means "to convict, refute", generally with a suggestion of the shame of the person convicted. This is the basis for teaching God's Word to expose the error of false teachers. Whenever this occurs, the one exposing the error will generally receive the wrath of the false teacher. This is why Timothy was to be strong and unafraid.

The faithful Christian today who believes God's Word and will not compromise its teaching may be perceived by others as intolerant and even bigoted. For the believer to say something is true and something else is false opens the Christian to the wrath of society and to possible backlash within the church as well. The audacity that a Christian who believes the Bible would claim to know truth for certain upsets many people.

I'm amazed at how tolerant professing Christians are of error today. The Evangelical Theological Society is a professional society of biblical scholars and theologians who affirm the inerrancy of Scripture. At least two of its members, Clark Pinnock, professor of theology at McMaster Divinity School, and John Sanders, associate professor of philosophy and religion at Huntington College, embraced an unorthodox view of God called "open theism." Some evangelical theologians in the Society believe this view to be heresy. In short, open theism is the view that God cannot know what will happen in the future, since future human decisions have not been made and are yet unknown until they are made.

When the Evangelical Theological Society met in November 2001, the Society voted overwhelmingly to reject open theism and affirm the foreknowledge of God. The vote was 253 in favor and 66 opposed, with 41 abstentions.[180] The major advocates, Clark Pinnock and John Sanders, continued to press their case. When the Society met in its annual meeting in the fall of 2003, another vote was taken. The vote this time was whether to expel these two high-profile proponents of open theism. After some debate the vote was taken; both men were sustained in their memberships in the Society. The two-thirds majority vote needed to expel fell short.[181] How ironic! The theology of open theism is flatly rejected as unbiblical, yet the proponents of the unbiblical theology are not censured.

Local churches are filled with such ironies as well. Members will fight over the smallest things that have nothing to do with doctrine. On what side should the piano be placed? What color do we paint the walls in the fellowship hall? The music is too loud or the temperature is too cold. These things can keep a congregation in turmoil. Yet these same members will embrace a teacher or a book that teaches error and think nothing of it!

The Holy Scriptures are also for correction. Reproof is to expose error and declare what is wrong. Correction is to declare what is right. The faithful Christian must do both. You would think that if a preacher today declared something to be right, the people could discern what is wrong. However, many people do not view moral opposites as one being right and the other being wrong. They simply view them to be different.

Take marriage, for instance. When a preacher says that biblically a marriage is between one man and one woman, one would discern then that the union of two men does not constitute a marriage. After hearing the preacher, some would not view one as right and the other wrong but both as right but different. This is when clear biblical application needs to be made.

Paul exhorts Timothy to give people what they need, not necessarily what they want. This was to be done with great patience and biblical teaching which would result in a sound ministry. Compelling forces that want to chase every new idea will always be around, because people grow tired of the "old, old story" and want something fresh. These old truths are just as applicable today as they were in the first century.

Some people seem to be in a race for relevance in the modern church; they chase after all things new so they can be on the "cutting edge." Church leaders are falling over themselves to get the "latest and greatest" whatever. This is all done in an effort to be relevant. In the early years of Billy Graham's ministry a critic accused Graham of setting back religion 100 years. Graham's response was that he did indeed want to set religion back—not 100 years, but 1,900 years back to the Book of Acts.

Some believe relevance is linked to the latest technology used in worship or religious musical genre or most recent innovative idea. The talk around the table at the local pastors' conference is generally about these subjects. Church-growth networks conduct seminars on these topics as well. The race for relevance is also pursued by those that sacrifice biblical authority for political correctness. A church that holds to "that old-time religion" is not considered relevant today. Those chasing after church relevance embrace most of the changing views of society. This is seen in women's issues, homosexual rights, environmental concerns, social justice, and correct speech. Words such as sin, hell, adultery, and others are to be excised from the Christian's vocabulary, particularly the preacher's. They are too offensive. In this day of "tolerance" the only thing not tolerated is a first-century kind of Jesus-follower. When you think about that, the first-century Christians were not tolerated then as well!

A contextualization confusion also goes on today. The effort to sound relevant and contextualize Christianity often results in cheapening our faith in the eyes of the world and minimizing the Gospel message. If Christians believe they have to act and look like the world to witness to others, they misunderstand contextualization. For example, some erroneously think that if a non-believer is drinking alcohol, the believer must imbibe as well to "be real" to the unbeliever. This is contextualization run amuck.

The last of Paul's parting advice to Timothy is to *do the work of an evangelist.*[182] Be a faithful witness. King Solomon declared, *The fruit of the righteous is a tree of life, And he who wins souls is wise.*[183] Jesus commanded us to take the Gospel to every nation. People are willing to go across the world to share their faith but are reluctant to go across the street to testify to the loving grace of Jesus Christ.

97

The spiritual discipline of witnessing needs to be cultivated in Christian lives today. Paul reminds the Christians in Corinth, *For we must all appear before the judgment seat of Christ, that each one may receive the things done in the body, according to what he has done, whether good or bad. Knowing, therefore, the terror of the Lord, we persuade men.*[184] We are called to be salt and light in this world. Salt irritates; light exposes the sins of our society. The cure is the redemption in Christ.

Timothy would fulfill his ministry by heeding Paul's words and implementing his advice. These truths are timeless and would benefit us as well. Paul's words establish a model for modern ministry. Paul could testify, *I have fought the good fight, I have finished the race, I have kept the faith*[185] because he practiced what he preached. We can do the same by staying true to God's Word.

Chapter 10

Standing Fast

Therefore, brethren, stand fast and hold the traditions which you were taught, whether by word or our epistle (2 Thess. 2:15).

During the last century our world has drastically changed. Futurists predict even greater changes will occur in the decades ahead. Consider the first manned flight that took place in Kitty Hawk, NC, by Orville and Wilbur Wright on December 17, 1903. That first propeller-driven airplane called the "Wright Flyer," flew for a grand total of 12 seconds. Almost eighty years later, on April 12, 1981, the first American space shuttle, "Columbia", was launched.

The first production Model T Ford was assembled in Detroit on October 1, 1908, without any of the accessories available today. Customers had one choice of color for their new car—black. Now we have a multitude of colors and styles from which to choose. Some of the latest updates include keyless automobiles with voice recognition software that respond to voice commands.

The development and use of antibiotic drugs today is commonplace. These are used to treat a number of what are now common health issues and to prevent diseases. Antibiotics are a relatively recent discovery. Penicillin was discovered by the Scottish scientist Sir Alexander Fleming in 1928 but was not readily available for the public until the 1940s. Advances in modern medicine have accelerated so quickly that today organ-transplant surgeries are becoming routine events. The potential for future use of medicine and medical technology changes daily.

Change is rapidly taking place all around us. We live in a mobile society. Almost one-third of the population in the United States moves every year; this effects people's sense of stability. In the midst of change, stability is a quality that is lacking and desperately needed in all of our lives. Government officials talk about stabilizing a staggering economy. Residential and commercial builders are responsible for constructing stable homes and office buildings. Ships of all types require stabilizers to counter the high winds and turbulent waters. Airplanes are built with stabilizers to help manage air turbulence. Our social structure functions best when people are stable and balanced. People with stable convictions are generally admired and stand out among others because of their consistency.

In his letters to the Christians in Thessalonica the Apostle Paul addresses the issue of stability. He had a serious concern for their spiritual welfare and the steadfastness of their faith. He sent Timothy to establish and encourage them about their faith. Paul did not want their faith *shaken by these afflictions*.[186] A few months later Paul wrote a second letter to them and addressed the same issue. He told them *not to be soon shaken in mind or troubled, either by spirit or by word or by letter, as if from us, as though the day of Christ had come*.[187] Concluding this admonition he wrote, *Therefore, brethren, stand fast and hold the traditions which you were taught, whether by word or our epistle*.[188]

Referring to Himself and the principles of His Word, Jesus taught that we are to be wise and build our lives on the rock of stability. Using a contrasting metaphor, Jesus declared that only a *foolish man* constructs his life upon the shifting sands of worldly wisdom and human philosophy.[189] Christ is the source of the believer's life and the foundation of its stability. When the unknown and insecurities of life move against us, we can plant our feet on the Rock of Ages to find stability and strength.

Paul identifies threats to stability in the Christian life; he encourages believers to stand against each one of them. One threat was persecution. He reminds the Thessalonian believers, *And you became followers of us and of the Lord, having received the word in much affliction, with joy of the Holy Spirit.*[190] Paul sent Timothy to them *to establish you and encourage you concerning your faith, that no one should be shaken by these afflictions; for you yourselves know that we are appointed to this. For, in fact, we told you before when we were with you that we would suffer tribulation, just as it happened, and you know.*[191]

False teaches comprised the second danger to their stability in the faith. Paul warned believers *not to be soon shaken in mind or troubled, either by spirit or by word or by letter, as if from us, as though the day of Christ had come. Let no one deceive you by any means.*[192] False teachers were entering into the church and using deceitful doctrine to influence many. The stability of individuals and the congregation as a whole was at risk.

Paul saw an additional threat to their spiritual stability in the area of temptation. He illustrated this warning by using the historical account of Moses and the children of Israel in the wilderness. *Therefore let him who thinks he stands take heed lest he fall. No temptation has overtaken you except such as is common to man; but God is faithful, who will not allow you to be tempted beyond what you are able, but with the temptation will also make the way of escape, that you may be able to bear it.*[193]

Our adversary, the devil, and the enemies of God are responsible for engendering instability and creating havoc in the Christian life. Instability can cause a believer to lose his testimony and bring shame to the name of Christ and reproach to His church. Current and future attacks will be physical in the area of persecution, intellectual in the area of false teachers, and morally affected by temptation. Paul warns that attacks in these areas will gradually rise to a climatic crescendo when the Anti-Christ is revealed. *Do you not remember that when I was still with you I told you these things?*[194]

Realizing the times and not wanting the believers to be led astray. Paul encourages them to stand firm. *Therefore, brethren, stand fast and hold the traditions which you were taught, whether by word or our epistle.*[195] Life issues today, in many ways, are not unlike what they were in the Paul's day. Therefore, these wise words from the Apostle still hold true for us as well.

Stand fast is translated from the Greek verb *steko,* which means "to be stationary." It is from *histemi,* a prolonged form of a primary *stao*, "to stand."[196] To more fully understand what Paul is saying, consider the word translated "falling away" in the same context of Paul's admonition.[197] "Falling away" is translated from *apostasia* that the English word "apostasy" is from. *Apostasia* is from *apo,* which means "away, or off", and *histemi,* a prolonged form of a primary *stao*, "to stand." *Apostasia* means "to stand away from."[198] Paul is telling the believers to "stand firm" in the faith and to hold to the things you have been taught, because some will be shaken in their faith and will "stand away from" those things.

Greater difficulties will be experienced by the church before the Lord's return. False teachers in the church will continue and will lead many astray. They will claim their teaching is from Paul when it is not. As a result, some will have their faith shattered; this will cause them to turn away from Christ and reject the truth they had once affirmed.

The spiritual condition of some mainline denominations in the United States is dreadful, because the teachings of Paul and other biblical writers have not been practiced. In a scathing newspaper article Charlotte Allen has exposed the problem. She writes, "The accelerating fragmentation of the strife-torn Episcopal Church USA, in which several parishes and even a few dioceses are opting out of the church, isn't simply about gay bishops, the blessing of same-sex unions or the election of a woman as presiding bishop. It also is about the meltdown of liberal Christianity . . . all but a few die-hards now admit, all the mainline churches and movements within churches that have blurred doctrine and softened moral precepts are demographically declining and, in the case of the Episcopal Church, disintegrating."[199]

The stability of the churches is determined by their adherence to the *faith once delivered to the saints*. False teachers spreading error can run through a church and a denomination like a virus spreads in a family. "Following the Episcopalian lead, the Presbyterians also voted to give local congregations the freedom to ordain openly cohabiting gay and lesbian ministers and endorsed the legalization of medical marijuana . . . . The Presbyterian Church USA is famous for its 1993 conference, cosponsored with the United Methodist Church, the Evangelical Lutheran Church in America, and other mainline churches, in which participants 'reimagined' God as 'Our Maker Sophia' and held a feminist-inspired 'milk and honey' ritual designed to replace traditional bread-and-wine Communion."[200]

Doctrine does matter; it is vital to the stability of a person's faith and the health of a congregation. "When your religion says 'whatever' on doctrinal matters, regards Jesus as just another wise teacher, refuses on principle to evangelize and lets you do pretty much what you want, it's a short step to deciding that one of the things you don't want to do is get up on Sunday morning and go to church."[201]

We are to stay true to the truth of Christ's return. In the first century, Paul warned about false teachers who said the day of Christ had already happened. This caused some to be shaken in their faith. The promise of Christ's return has forever been a stabilizing influence in the church. To think this event has already passed would tear apart the belief system of His followers.

Some scoffers today chide at the idea that Christ will return. Many unknowingly mimic the scoffers in the first century as they question, *"Where is the promise of His coming? For since the fathers fell asleep, all things continue as they were from the beginning of creation."*[202] Though the return of Christ has been delayed, He still will return as He promised. His delay has allowed time for many people to repent of their sins and commit their lives to follow Christ.

Paul is also telling the Thessalonian believers to stand firm to the truth of salvation. God has called us in Christ by the Holy Spirit to believe the truth and to live holy lives. Salvation truth is clearly spelled out in Scripture. Jesus Christ Himself declared that he is the only way of salvation.[203] The Apostle Peter declared the same truth by saying, *Nor is there salvation in any other, for there is no other name under heaven given among men by which we must be saved.*[204] This has been the historic Christian truth since the beginning of the church and is that *tradition* that Paul says to *stand fast* and to hold to.

Sadly, many of the mainline denominations have strayed from this truth. Instead of confessing the exclusivity of Christ in salvation they have opened the door to error and confessed Jesus to be one way among many. Methodist Bishop Joseph

Sprague is illustrative of the doublespeak of many denominational leaders about the exclusive claims of Christ in salvation. Bishop Sprague will affirm the language of the ancient creeds yet at the sam time, deny them. Addressing the Iliff School of Theology in Denver, CO, he said, "I must dissent from Christocentric exclusives which hold that Jesus is the only way to God's gift of salvation. Such an arrogant claim stands over and against the inclusive Jesus of the synoptics and limits God in ways that humans cannot and must not."[205]

The exhortation by Paul to the Christians in Thessalonica was twofold. They were to stand firm to the truth of Christ's return and to His claim of salvation. They also were to stay faithful to the traditions they had been taught. Paul is warning that gale-force winds of danger will blow believers off their feet and away to destruction should they not anchor themselves to solid ground. Paul had seen these gale-force winds of persecution from the culture and false teachings in the church. This is the reason for his plea to *stand fast and hold the traditions which you were taught, whether by word or our epistle.*[206]

The verbs *stand* and *hold* are both present tense, which conveys continual action. The concept of "keep on standing" and "keep on holding" is the better understanding of Paul's exhortation. His word to those first-century believers, as well as to us, is to keep holding onto the traditions or what he has taught. *Traditions* is translated from the Greek word *paradosis*. This compound word is from *para*, which means "near, beside" and *didomi*, a primary verb "to give" or "to hand over" or "deliver." Thus *paradosis* is truth, which having been received, must be faithfully handed down.

All things "traditional" in modern culture and particularly in contemporary church life are considered anathema. The mantra espoused by church leaders today almost seems to be reflected in the saying, "Throw out the old and bring in the new." Most contemporary churches place little or no value on tradition. Most undervalue tradition. Jaroslav Pelican called tradition "the living faith of the dead" and traditionalism "the dead faith of the living." Tradition continues to live in an ongoing conversation with the past. The tradition Paul references is the teaching the church has received from him whether in person or by letter. The doctrine he taught is to be held tightly and passed to succeeding generations of believers. Paul's oral instructions were given when he was present with them. Much of the apostolic teaching was passed down from previous generations by oral tradition.

The letters that he wrote to the first-century churches now make up a majority of the New Testament. The apostolic teachings are foundation to the doctrines of the Christian faith. What was taught in the early church, either by word or letter, is what Christian churches should be teaching today. To follow Paul's admonition to stay faithful and hold onto the teachings is synonymous to a biblical Christian.

Adhering to the teachings of Christ and the apostles without compromise brings stability to the Christian life. We are not to pick and choose what to believe. We are to believe in the entire Bible. Churches and denominations today that have abandoned the teachings of Christ and the apostles are in serious decline. Rejecting the authority of the Bible and the teachings of Scripture cannot and will not ever lead to stable Christian lives.

The Word of God will never be embraced by many in our culture and society. The more a church endeavors to be relevant and "soft-sells" the Gospel, the less stable it will become. Not all people are looking for God's revelation to us. People are looking for a sure Word of God. Solid Bible teaching in the church develops Christian stability and strengthens the believer to withstand the pressures of persecution, false teaching, and temptation.

My prayer for you would parallel that of the Apostle's: *Now may our Lord Jesus Christ Himself, and our God and Father, who has loved us and given us everlasting consolation and good hope by grace, comfort your hearts and establish you in every good word and work.*[207]

Chapter 11

Counter-Culture Christians

Now this is the testimony of John, when the Jews sent priests and Levites from Jerusalem to ask him, "Who are you?" He confessed, and did not deny, but confessed, "I am not the Christ." And they asked him, "What then? Are you Elijah?" He said, "I am not." "Are you the Prophet?" And he answered, "No." Then they said to him, "Who are you, that we may give an answer to those who sent us? What do you say about yourself? "He said: "I am 'The voice of one crying in the wilderness: 'Make straight the way of the LORD,'"' as the prophet Isaiah said"
(John 1:19-23).

John the Baptist was a different kind of preacher. He was the forerunner of Jesus, whose mission was foretold by Isaiah, *The voice of one crying in the wilderness: "Prepare the way of the Lord; Make straight in the desert a highway for our God*[208,] and Malachi, *"Behold, I send My messenger, And he will prepare the way before Me."*[209] John reminded many people in his day of the prophet Elijah because of his impetuosity and firebrand preaching. He was a fearless preacher as he called for politicians[210] and religious leaders[211] as well as common people to repent.[212] His life was characterized not only by holy courage but also self-denial and humility.[213] For his courage to speak the truth he became a willing victim to prison and even death.

Baptists throughout their history have held John the Baptist in high esteem for his boldness to proclaim the Word of God. Some have even attempted to trace Baptists' roots back to the John the Baptist. These attempts have fallen short and been rejected by historians. Although no "trail of blood" line of succession can be articulated, Baptist do have some things in common with this individualistic forerunner of Jesus. Baptists are dissenters and have a long history of dissent. Historically, Baptist preachers have been prophetic voices speaking to government officials about church-and-state separation. They have also stated their position opposing the established state church and revealed her abuses of doctrine and power. Baptists have separated themselves from other ecclesial groups by their doctrinal distinctives of regenerate church membership signified by baptism for believers only. This believers' church is also sustained by church discipline.

The identifying name *Baptist* originally was a term of derision their critics gave them because of the way they practiced baptism. Early Baptists were rejected by the established church and were viewed skeptically by the state. They were historically a counter-culture people going against the grain of both church and state. Their refusal to conform to the culture of the day caused them to be viewed as outcasts. Because of their insistence on the authority of the Bible to guide them in matters of faith and practice, they were greatly persecuted and even put to death.

An illustration of the animosity toward those that insisted on practicing the teachings of the New Testament is Balthasar Hubmaier (1480-1528), a 16th century reformer and Anabaptist leader. He met Ulrich Zwingli on a trip to Zurich in 1523. Zwingli organized a group of young men to study the Greek New Testament together. After much study a sense grew in the group that the established church teachings were not true to the New Testament text. Zwingli began to press the government leaders to replace the Roman Catholic Church with a Reformed church. After his success, a schism began to develop within the group. Hubmaier and some others wanted to press for further reforms in stopping the practice of baptizing infants and only baptize those adults who were old enough to understand the commitment they were making to Christ.

The city officials were troubled with all that was happening and prohibited the group from meeting. Hubmaier then moved to Austria and began to be pastor of the church at Waldshut. He continued to follow the practices of the New Testament and went against the established church teaching. The Austrian Army captured the city in 1525. Hubmaier fled back to Zurich and hoped for help from Zwingli but instead was arrested. Hubmaier was tortured and partially recanted his beliefs, which he later regretted and retracted, and left Switzerland.

In 1527 he and his wife were arrested by King Ferdinand's men and extradited to Vienna, where he was tried as a heretic and condemned. He was burned at the stake in Vienna on March 10, 1528. Three days after his execution, a stone was tied around his wife's neck; she was thrown into the Danube River to drown.[214]

Many of our Baptist forefathers were martyred by drowning. This was an insidious way by the established church to ridicule their biblical view of baptism and to rid the church of so-called heretics. One particular method of drowning was described by attaching an iron chain to a heavy stone. Both the person and the weight to which the individual was fastened were then laid on a plank. The ends of the plank were placed on two boats, which were rowed out on the water. Then the boats separated; the weight of the martyr sank to the bottom.

One such martyr was Anthony Ricetti, a Protestant and a

citizen of Venice. History records his story. "A few days before his execution his son went to him, and begged him to recant, that his life might be saved, and himself not left an orphan. To this the father replied, 'A true Christian is bound to give up not only goods and children, but life itself, for the glory of his Redeemer.' The nobles of Venice offered him his life if he would change his religion; but finding their efforts unavailing, they ordered the execution of his sentence which took place accordingly."[215] Ricetti was then drowned because of the testimony of his faith and his convictions in the Word of God.

John the Baptist was a counter-culture preacher such as these who sacrificed their lives for the Gospel. The Scriptures reveal that John the Baptist was a great preacher with widespread fame. *Then Jerusalem, all Judea, and all the region around the Jordan went out to him and were baptized by him in the Jordan, confessing their sins.*[216] Even King Herod respected John the Baptist; he believed him to be a *holy man* and *heard him gladly.*[217] When the Baptist pointed out the biblically unlawful relationship between the King and his brother's wife, Herodias, the political pressure became too great for Herod to resist. He therefore ordered the head of John the Baptist on a platter as Herodias desired.[218]

A great lesson revealed in this biblical story can be learned by all counter-culture preachers. As long as a man of God doesn't take a strong stand against the sins of government officials, he will not be criticized or perceived to be out of step with the mainstream. If the preacher panders to the politician, he will typically receive great endorsement and greater respect. If the preacher calls attention to the sin and corruption of an official, he might risk his popularity, his ministry, and even his life physically.

Jesus had high regard for this itinerant, colorful preacher. Our Lord gave John the Baptist one of the highest compliments possible. He declared, *"Assuredly, I say to you, among those born of women there has not risen one greater than John the Baptist."*[219] He was a prophet to the culture and often resembled the ministry of Elijah. Wherever he traveled, the religious leaders would interrogate him about his ministry. The questions asked of John the Baptist by those unknown to him are similar to the ones Baptists have historically answered to justify their existence. Reviewing these questions in our modern society is beneficial. A thorough, inward examination will determine if we have stayed true to the faith of our forefathers or whether we have abandoned our doctrinal distinctives on the altar of ecumenism.

The first question asked of John the Baptist was *"Who are you?"*[220] After four centuries of Christian witness the Baptist movement still must define itself to contemporary culture. People still want to know who we are. Though Baptists are stronger in the southern regions of the United States, many still do not know them.

Baptists have advanced within society only when they have spoken prophetically to the popular culture and to the larger Christian world. In true Reformation tradition, the early Baptists put into practice what they believed the Bible clearly taught. Anabaptists are considered the first to baptize biblically by immersion. Since the practice of infant baptism was pervasive in that day, this baptism was called a *rebaptism*. These bold believers swam against the tide of the church and culture. Some gave their lives in contending for this truth. "Because some connected with the Anabaptist movement on the Continent and refused to see themselves as proper subjects of civil government, the epithet, Anabaptist, when applied to English Baptists and implying a rebellious and anarchistic spirit, was vigorously rejected. While their influence on the broader Baptist movement is not well documented, their influence on John Smyth and Thomas Helwys is indisputable."[221] Some cultural curiosities today want to know who are these Baptists. We should respond to those queries with a clear delineation of our biblical distinctives. All too often, however, we are witnessing the very opposite take place. Instead of clearly stating who we are, many Baptist churches are camouflaging their Baptist distinctives to accommodate the culture. The result is misleading and confusing. Paul admonished believers to speak clearly. *Even things without life, whether flute or harp, when they make a sound, unless they make a distinction in the sounds, how will it be known what is piped or played? For if the trumpet makes an uncertain sound, who will prepare for battle?*[222] This concealing identity is done in a so-called effort to be relevant so the church will grow.

The people from Jerusalem were curious about John the Baptist and confused as to who he might be. Some thought he might be Elijah, the Old Testament prophet, or the Christ. They were puzzled as to his identity. John was quick to make very clear in the strongest terms who he was. *He confessed, and did not deny, but confessed, "I am not the Christ." And they asked him, "What then? Are you Elijah?" He said, "I am not." "Are you the Prophet?" And he answered, "No." Then they said to him, "Who are you, that we may give an answer to those who sent us? What do you say about yourself?" He said: "I am 'The voice of one crying in the wilderness: "Make straight the way of the Lord,"' as the prophet Isaiah said."*[223] He was very transparent and did not try to camouflage who he was or what his purpose was.

This is a great lesson for Baptists today. We would do well to clearly identify ourselves to the larger culture. Many established Baptist churches are removing the identifying label *Baptist* from their church names. These new contemporary names make no reference whatsoever that the church is a

113

Baptist church. The present trend in starting new churches follows this pattern as well. These new church starts are funded with Baptist money, but the church planters make it clear that the word *Baptist* will not be in the name. This tendency to camouflage the real identity of the church is rationalized as necessary for church growth. If the Baptist name is a hindrance for church growth, then one would conclude that all church starts without the Baptist name would grow. But that is not the case at all. In fact, almost one-third of new church starts do not survive four years. Ed Stetzer, former senior director of the North American Mission Board's Center for Missional Research and presently director of LifeWay Research, reports, "We found that the survivability rate of the church plants in our study was 68 percent after four years—and this was similar in all denominations."[224]

The research by Stetzer included different denominations, not just Baptists. The results would suggest that camouflaging denominational identity does not ensure survivability or rapid growth of the church. If concealing the Baptist identity of a church does not guarantee growth, then why not disclose the denomination of the church? Hiding the type of church seems to suggest more of a softening of convictions about Baptist distinctives. The latter appears to fit better within the context of today's post-modern culture.

The Southern Baptist Convention looks a lot different today than it did 100 years ago. Though many things have changed throughout the last century, the denominational concerns are the same. "With the coming of the new century, Southern Baptists prepared to face the future with renewed commitment and great expectations. This was also a time when leaders of the denomination felt the need to emphasize Baptist distinctives and denominational identity in the face of growing pluralism and increasing diversity across the religious landscape,"[225] wrote J. M. Frost, founder of the Baptist Sunday School Board. The need Frost saw last century was to advance Baptist distinctives and denominational identity. This is the same need today. The trend toward ecumenism is diminishing doctrinal differences. To find common theological ground one has to retreat to the lowest common denominator and sacrifice biblical distinctives. Baptists need to get more serious about their doctrinal distinctives and quit trying to be an ecclesial supermarket serving the whims of religious consumers.

The second question people had about John the Baptist was to know his purpose and mission. The Bible tells us, *There was a man sent from God, whose name was John. This man came for a witness, to bear witness of the Light, that all through him might believe. He was not that Light, but was sent to bear witness of that Light.*[226] John understood his purpose very well and lived his life fulfilling his mission.

Contemporary Baptists are struggling today to find themselves. "The old-time religion" seems too outdated for fashionable Baptists in present-day society and too offensive for their fragile egos. What seems fashionable today is for Baptists to remake themselves to be more palatable to postmodern people. "What was judged true and wise yesterday," writes David Wells, "must now be passé, that anything on the cutting edge must necessarily be superior. And we persist in this delusion despite the fact that the lives of us moderns, with our historically unprecedented wealth of knowledge, are everywhere characterized by emptiness, superficiality, banality, and destructiveness, whereas the lives of those who lived in previous ages and knew so much less than we do today were often comparatively more human, more serious, and more profound."[227] In this frenzy to find themselves, many have lost their way all together.

John the Baptist was sent from God to do ministry. The call of God into the ministry is a bedrock belief of Baptists. Pastors and church leaders give all kinds of reasons why they go into the ministry. Some want to help people. Others think it is a noble profession. The true calling of God should include a concern about others, particularly their spiritual condition, but the call of God on a person's life into the ministry is what ultimately matters. Addressing the call of God on the preacher, Martyn Lloyd-Jones writes, "I would say that the only man who is called to preach is the man who cannot do anything else, in the sense that he is not satisfied with anything else. This call to preach is so put upon him, and such pressure comes to bear upon him that he says, 'I can do nothing else, I must preach.'"[228]

The summons of God on an individual to preach the Word of God will sustain the minister in difficult times. This divine call is not anything new but is rooted within Scripture. Isaiah experienced his call after the death of King Uzziah.[229] Jeremiah responded to his call of God in his youth yet thought he was too young. He was informed that God called him even before he was born.[230] Ezekiel received his call from God after a vision of the future.[231] Down through the years to the present time Baptists have adhered to the call of God as a prerequisite to the ministry.

John the Baptist was called by God to bear witness to the Light, Jesus Christ. When questioned about his mission he said very clearly who he was and who he was not. People were to have no doubt in their minds. He plainly stated that he was *"not the Christ."* He was not Elijah nor the Prophet.[232] John also positively affirmed what he was about. *He said, "I am 'The voice of one crying in the wilderness: "'Make straight the way of the Lord,'"' as the prophet Isaiah said."*[233]

The way John responded to his questioners should be the

way modern-day Baptists identify themselves. A clear delineation should say who Baptists are and who they are not. Baptists are not a hodgepodge of everything evangelical. They have clear biblical distinctives. Evangelicalism, however, is losing its theological moorings because it has not been clear about its doctrine. Peter Leithart explains, "Evangelicals entered the mainstream of American life during the late 1970s and 'almost immediately' lost their ability to define themselves theologically. Modernity's separation of public and private has limited evangelicals' beliefs 'to matters of private experience, increasingly shorn of their distinctive worldview, and increasingly withdrawn from what was external and public.' Ultimately, 'being evangelical has come to mean simply that one has had a certain kind of religious experience that gives color to the private aspects of daily life but in which few identifiable theological elements can be discerned or, as it turns out, are necessary.'"[234]

The antidote for Baptists to not travel the same path of Evangelicalism is to remain true to their doctrinal distinctives. Celebrate them and adhere to them, or the same fate of Evangelicalism will be ours. Peter Leithart observes, "Spend a little time among evangelicals, and you are sure to learn about people who believe all the right doctrine but are not 'real' — which is to say, born-again—Christians."[235] This is lamentable to say the least. The hesitancy to declare Baptist distinctives is based on the premise that the unchurched do not want doctrine but their felt-needs met. David Wells offers great insight to this idea. "It is surely ironic that those who seek to promote the church have adopted strategies that deliberately obscure its essence. The church should be known as a place where God is worshiped, where the Word of God is heard and practiced, and where life is thought about and given its most searching and serious analysis. This, in fact, is what the traditional church has seen as its chief business, however badly it may have been doing this business. But none of this can be marketed, and so it is ignored. The interest turns to how well appointed and organized the church is, what programs it has to offer, how many outings the youth group has organized, how convenient it is to attend, how good the nursery is. The truly important matters are marginalized and the marginal aspects of the life of the church are made central."[236]

The religious leaders also questioned John the Baptist about his authority. What right did he have to preach? What authority did he have to baptize or to carry forth his ministry? *"And they asked him, saying, 'Why then do you baptize if you are not the Christ, nor Elijah, nor the Prophet?'"*[237] Our authority is from God, as revealed in the Holy Scriptures. The question of authority is a relevant question for Baptists today because of the individualistic nature of the post-modern individual. The trend today is to elevate the individual view as supreme over anything else. Truth is seen as subjective and personal, without any real objective basis. "The constant cultural bombardment of individualism, in the absence of a robust theology, meant that faith that had rightly been understood as personal now easily became faith that was individualistic, self-focused, and consumer oriented.[238] Therefore, whatever interpretation a person has about a passage of Scripture is what that verse means.

This line of thinking is contrary to the Word of God. "Knowing this first, that no prophecy of Scripture is of any private interpretation, for prophecy never came by the will of man, but holy men of God spoke as they were moved by the Holy Spirit".[239] Biblical interpretation is not a subjective private exercise but is bound by the Word of God and supported by the confessional theology of the church. Otherwise, one interpretation would be as valid as another; the opinions of the individual would override the church's confessional statements. An individual interpretation could then "deny the confession any official value. Thus, a creed may be made creedless while creedlessness may be given creedal status."[240] The results would be disastrous; no definitive way would exist to discern truth from error.

John the Baptist also was questioned as to his message. He explodes on the biblical scene preaching, *"Repent, for the kingdom of heaven is at hand!"*[241] He came preaching, not story-telling nor leading a discussion group. He declared people were sinners and needed to repent. True repentance is more than lip service and would be seen in the actions of an individual.[242]

In the modern church this kind of preaching is in short supply. Repentance from sin is seldom declared from church pulpits, if they have one. The therapist's couch has replaced the pulpit in some churches. Felt-needs such as obtaining happiness, overcoming loneliness, dealing with depression, and gaining material wealth are typical of the messages of the day. Felt-needs have trumped biblical doctrine in the preaching ministry. In this therapeutic culture, sin is treated as a disease and not as wickedness and rebellion against God. At the center of our culture is the assumption that all of us are either in therapy or in denial. Every mood, every feeling or relationship is rooted in some syndrome that must be cured by therapy or psychotropic drugs. All of us have needs, but great caution must be made to not interpret these needs ourselves. Every need should be seen in light of our broken relationship with God. For many the problem is sin; the cure is repentance.

John preached the Word of God. Too many preachers think what the Gospel needs is more clearer, novel presentations. What the Gospel really needs is to be proclaimed in its simple purity. The message of repentance calls people to turn from themselves to Christ. The "autonomous self" must die that Christ may take charge of the life. It is a difficult but necessary message.

Jim Bakker, the head of a multi-million dollar religious empire known as Heritage USA, now fully admits he was wrong. In fact, the title of his 1996 book is *I Was Wrong*. Bakker preached a prosperity gospel that reached out to the felt needs of his audience. Now he fully admits that he omitted the more difficult teachings of the Bible. His selfish ambition coupled with his message led to his conviction in 1989 of 24 counts of defrauding the public. He was sentenced to 45 years in prison and a $500,000 fine; he served almost five years before being paroled. While he was in prison, he spent time reading and studying the Scriptures. He studied a book he thought he already knew, but he now says that the study changed his life. Now he says that he has a different ministry—one that includes repentance.

Repentance is a counter-cultural message. It is a biblical message. John the Baptist, a counter-cultural preacher, declared it. This world needs to witness believers that do not "go with the flow" but are willing to go counter to the culture. This is who Baptists have historically been. It is who we need to be today!

Chapter 12

The Changing Face of the Church

Now I beseech you therefore, brethren, by the
mercies of God, that you present your bodies a
living sacrifice, holy, acceptable to God, which is your reason-
able service. And do not be conformed to this world, but be
transformed by the renewing of your mind, that you may prove
what is that good and acceptable and perfect will of God
*(*Rom. 12:1-2*).*

Change is a fact of life. Someone once said that the only
constant in life is change. Change is taking place at a rapid
pace in our society; the church is not exempt from this development. Worship in many churches today would not be recog-
nizable by our grandparents' generation. Past generations
would be totally shocked to see what is taking place in some
of the churches they once attended. Sociologists have studied
this movement for several decades and have offered a variety
of theories as to why it is happening. Futurists suggest what
the church and society will look like in the next decades.
Church growth experts endeavor to syncretize these findings to
apply to the churches. Pastors propose ways to implement the
findings into the life of the church. The people in the congregation become bewildered and question the prudence of the
change.

No doubt exists about whether the church is changing. The
question is about the degree of needed change. Change does

not necessarily mean progress, but progress will necessitate change. Even though churches are changing, Christianity as a whole remains strong. "Indeed, the mistake some people make is to interpret a decline in particular institutions (such as mainline Protestantism or the Roman Catholic Church) as implying the demise of religion more generally."[243] Change in itself is neither good nor bad. The nature of the change will more specifically determine its virtue.

Paul, in writing to the church at Rome, references these two types of change. *Do not be conformed to the world*[244] is the kind of change the believer should avoid. However, *be transformed by the renewing of your mind*[245] is the change to which every Christian should aspire. The change taking place in many of our churches is the result of change taking place in our belief systems. Churches have incrementally transformed their practice to justify and emulate their changing theology.

The influence of the culture has significantly impacted the theology and practice of the church. Churches, reflecting the theology of her leaders, have abandoned the authority of the Bible and substituted the prevailing cultural attitudes. The influence of the women's movement has led to the ordination of women pastors in evangelical churches. The changing attitude toward normalization of homosexuality within society continues to shape the church's outlook as well. Finding denominations as a whole affirming homosexual "marriage" and ordaining homosexuals to serve as pastors is not uncommon today.

Paul exhorts the believers in Rome not to "fashion oneself" according to the world. The Apostle Peter uses the same word when he says, *as obedient children, not conforming yourselves to the former lusts, as in your ignorance.*[246] The advice is not to shape ourselves after the lusts of the flesh or the attitudes of the world which is ungodly but after holiness and the will of

God. Sociologist James Hunter has observed these changes and their impact on Evangelicalism. "The social transformation that occurred within American society in the past century owning to the augmentation of the modernizing forces have been astonishing. The consequences of these changes for Evangelicalism have been equally traumatic. Overall, conservative Protestantism has gone from a position of cultural dominance and institutional power to varying levels of cultural subordination and social-structural insignificance . . .. Evangelicalism has as a result of its encounter with the modernizing forces undergone its own inner transformation."[247] Many churches today are disregarding these admonitions.

The cultural impact on the church can be seen in several critical areas. One is commitment signified by the lack of dedication to the local church by her members. Membership is viewed more casually today in most churches; less is expected of members. Some churches may require new members to sign cards outlining membership requirements, but rarely are those conditions enforced. Church discipline has been generally abandoned in the modern church. At the same time, some churches hold to an even higher commitment of expectations of her members. These churches are generally making more of an impact in their communities. They actually are the exception in today's world.

The growing trend is to downplay commitment to the local church because the local church is perceived to be THE problem. Reggie McNeal is one of these proponents. He writes, "In every arena I am running into an increasing number of people who are expressing fundamental doubts about the viability of the church. These are not critics from the outside who don't like what the church is doing. These are connected leaders who don't like what they are experiencing in church."[248] This is the rationale that has caused some to conclude that to save their faith, they have had to abandon the church.[249]

No one would suggest that the local church doesn't have problems. Certainly no church is perfect. Challenges have always existed within local churches. False doctrine, poor leadership, unregenerate members, carnality, and worldliness are some of the issues the New Testament addresses. The church does not consist of bricks and mortar but of flesh and blood. Some problems in the church will always exist, because people with problems are in the church. *Christ loved the church and gave Himself for her.*[250] For a person to confess to be a Christian and yet not to love the things that Jesus loved appears inconsistent. He loved the church and was committed to her. Every believer should do the same.

Many would affirm their love for the church universal but their disdain for the local church. Organized religion is what they are against. They would blame organized religion for almost all the evils in the world. They believe organized religion to be divisive and intolerant because it adheres to absolute truth claims that are repressive and discriminatory. Therefore, they tend to drop out or want no part of organized religion. Consider their alternative—unorganized religion!

Demanding a deeper commitment to the local church is not a viable solution by emerging network leaders. Being a "good church member" has failed in their view. As a result they have now redefined what a "good church member" is. The answer, then, is not reformation or correction but total abandonment. "I think the solution is an abandonment of the church culture idolatry and a radical reintroduction of spiritual formation," says McNeal.[251]

Another area the contemporary church has surrendered to culture is in the preaching ministry. Biblical preaching, particularly expository preaching, is in short supply today. The absence of preaching can be seen symbolically in some churches by the removal of the pulpit from the worship center. Certainly the presence of a pulpit does not guarantee biblical preaching will take place. And true, a preacher does not need a pulpit to declare the Word of God. The removal of the pulpit in a church is a strong symbolic statement that preaching does not have the same status in worship as it once had in the past.

The act of preaching in many churches today is considered "old school." The new trend is dialogue and conversation, storytelling and drama, interviews and film clips. Hollywood appears to have more stylistic influence on some modern preachers than does history. Some contemporary preachers are more interested in interpreting culture than in interpreting Scripture. The rationale for the change is that people are tired of monologue and want dialogue. "Today's sermons tend to be short, shallow, topical homilies that massage people's egos and focus on fairly insipid subjects like human relationships, 'successful' living, emotional issues, and other practical but worldly—and not definitely *biblical*—themes. Like the ubiquitous Plexiglas lecterns from which these messages are delivered, such preaching is lightweight and without substance, cheap and synthetic, leaving little more than an ephemeral impression on the minds of the hearers."[252]

Paul declared, *For since, in the wisdom of God, the world through wisdom did not know God, it pleased God through the foolishness of the message preached to save those who believe.*[253] Worldly wisdom cannot provide a suitable substitute for preaching. The declaration of the Word of God can be found throughout Scripture. The Old Testament prophets boldly declared God's Word to the people. Jesus preached, *"Repent for the kingdom of heaven is at hand."*[254] John the Baptist entered the scene preaching repentance. The disciples preached to the people in the cities. Preaching was a central component in spreading the Gospel of Christ.

Those that advocate a new approach avoid doctrinal preaching altogether. They prescribe that proclaiming the uniqueness and exclusivity of Christ, the demands of obedience, the reality of hell, the call to holiness, and the commands of evangelism and discipleship will only turn off people and drive them away from the church. This kind of biblical preaching, they claim, does not address the needs of the modern-day listener. It is too rigid and boring and not relevant to their lives. The preacher should simply dialogue with the congregation and tell the people stories about the humanity of Jesus so they can identify with Him and develop a relationship with Him. Doctrine is out and the relationship is deemed to be more important.

This type of "preaching" is viewed as relevant to modern man. Biblical language and theological terms should be avoided, because people do not understand them and they really have no meaning to us today. Communicating biblical truth requires clear and precise language. "The language can be bent only so far, till it is bent out of shape. The apostles of relevance do not see this problem, and hence toss away the truths they genuinely want to convey."[255] Biblical truth loses its meaning when, to be relevant, theological words are replaced with lesser words. Mark Twain is to have once said that the difference between the almost right word and the right word is really a large matter. It's the difference between the lightning bug and the lightning. "If the Christian revelation is both true and a truth to which fallen men are partly blinded, and a truth of great complexity and sophistication, a preacher may be most relevant when his language is least contemporary, and may be irrelevant to the point of fatuousness when it is most contemporary."[256]

The new approach to preaching also uses the Bible in a different way. Holy Scripture is not the foundation for propositional truth to be proclaimed but rather used to excite the imagination to connect us together through stories. Endeavoring to "teach" this new way Rob Bell says, "We're rediscovering Christianity as an Eastern religion, as a way of life. Legal metaphors for faith don't deliver a way of life."[257] Rob's wife, Kristen, also contributed her views to this new approach. "I grew up thinking that we've figured out the Bible," Kristen says, "that we knew what it means. Now I have no idea what most of it means. And yet I feel like life is big again—like life used to be black and white, and now it's in color."[258] In essence this new approach to preaching is really old-time liberalism.

Worship is also changing in the church today. Many churches have fought ungodly worship wars and have left behind a multitude of casualties. Some churches have become divided over this issue; church-staff members have even been dismissed. The turmoil created in many churches because of changing worship patterns reveals the very personal aspect of this act. The rise of individualism in America coupled with the growing diversity and the diminished view of local-church worship is becoming more personal and less corporate. Yet worship is both personal and corporate.

What is worship? The word *worship* is from an Old English compound word *worth* and *ship*. It means to ascribe or recognize worth. The worship of God is to ascribe His worth. The psalmist declared, *Give unto the Lord the glory due to His name; Worship the Lord in the beauty of holiness.*[259] And again *"Oh come, let us worship and bow down; Let us kneel before the Lord our Maker."*[260] God is worthy of our praise and adoration simply because of who He is.

The Bible does not leave us without direction in the worship of God. Jesus said to the woman at the well, *"God is Spirit, and those who worship Him must worship in spirit and truth.*"[261] Authentic worship can be possible only when we explore the depths of spiritual truth. God has revealed Himself in Holy Scripture. High and holy thoughts of God cannot be fully realized until the people of God have dug deep into the Word of God. Preaching that does not expound the revelation of God to humanity will not lead to true worship. Genuine worship does not take place apart from Bible-centered preaching.

The prophet Amos spoke to the children of Israel about their worship. His message revealed God's displeasure toward them and their vain worship. *Though you offer Me burnt offerings and your grain offerings, I will not accept them, Nor will I regard your fattened peace offerings. Take away from Me the noise of your songs, For I will not hear the melody of your stringed instruments.*[262] The prophet exposed the error of their worship. They thought if the externals of worship were performed, God would be satisfied. He was not and rejected their worship.

Worship is not simply about the externals of ritual but the internals of righteousness. King David knew this truth well when he declared, *For You do not desire sacrifice, or else I would give it; You do not delight in burnt offering. The sacrifices of God are a broken spirit, A broken and a contrite heart —These, O God, You will not despise.*[263] Innovative methods and avant-garde practices within some of the emergent-church movement will not constitute true worship of God.

The Jews in Jesus' time and the Samaritans debated the proper place for worship. A Samaritan woman at Jacob's well mentioned this to Jesus. *"Our fathers worshiped on this mountain, and you Jews say that in Jerusalem is the place where one ought to worship."*[264] The church today has an endless debate over similar issues such as when to take an offering in the service, who should lead the music, whether raising one's hands is acceptable, and a host of other questions. All these have to do with form rather than content. The content of worship is prayer, praise, doctrine, and theology. However, this formula is considered boring and irrelevant by many today. The solution, therefore, is to make church exciting and fun. This is the modern mantra.

The push to change worship today is all about form. Churches spend thousands of dollars on high-tech devices to appeal to the senses. Music videos, light shows, magic shows, bands, and other forms of entertainment are the menu entrees for worship. The best shows will draw the biggest crowds. This is a time in which modern-day church leaders are trying to build their congregations on entertainment. The words of Charles Spurgeon, the great English Baptist of the 19th century should be heeded. "This is the drift of the times. I can justify the broadest statement I have made by the action or by the speech of certain ministers, who are treacherously betraying our holy religion under pretense of adapting it to this progressive age. The new plan is to assimilate the church to the world, and so include a larger area within its bounds. By semi-dramatic performances they make houses of prayer to approximate to the theater. They turn their services into musical displays, and their sermons into political harangues or philosophical essays. In fact, they exchange the temple for the theater, and turn ministers of God into actors, whose business it is to amuse men."[265]

Coupled with the changing worship patterns are the changing musical styles in the church. Music has long been a part of the worship of God. *"Sing praise to the Lord, you saints of His, And give thanks at the remembrance of His holy name."*[266] Many today believe that worship is synonymous with singing. Although singing is a part of worship, it is not the totality of worship. Singing, however, seems to have taken center-stage in many typical Sunday church services. Preaching once was the centerpiece of the worship service. Today it is viewed as a separate aspect of worship and at times will intrude on the praise and worship time.

The contemporary music style so prevalent in the modern church has its roots in the Jesus Movement of the 1960s and 70s. The charismatic movement of the 1960s also has some residual effects on the church music today. Musical styles have changed throughout the years; today is really no different. Whether the content is doctrinally sound and the form honoring to God are the two great concerns with modern church music.

Historically a variety of styles in worship music have existed. High church, low church, traditional, contemporary, gospel, classical, and country are some of those forms. The modern church would add to the list various genres of rock music and rap. Whatever style a church would use, the content of the music should be doctrinally sound. The lyrics should be intelligible and easily understood.

The way the music is presented should be honoring to the Lord. People should see a clear distinction between the actions and manners of those attending a rock concert and those in a worship service. The music should prepare the congregation for the preaching of God's Word. Preaching is to be central to the worship of God, not secondary to the music. For the congregation to hear from God through His Word is vitally important. We need to hear from God more than we need to speak to Him. During the time of the Reformation, Martin Luther said, "Next to theology, I give the first place and the highest honor to music."[267] Music has its place in worship but not above the Word of God.

The rise of the megachurch also is a part of the changing landscape of the modern church. According to the *Mega-*

churches Today 2005[268] survey, at least 1,210 megachurches with an average weekly attendance of more than 3,600 are in the U.S. This is almost double the number of megachurches in existence in 2001. The definition of a megachurch is a congregation running 2,000 or more in attendance on a typical weekend.

A few megachurches have existed in the history of the church, but these have been nothing compared to the numbers we see today. The church at Jerusalem was evidently a megachurch, particularly since 3,000 people were saved on the day of Pentecost. Charles Haddon Spurgeon was pastor of the Metropolitan Tabernacle in London in the middle to late 19th century. For 37 years he was pastor of one church which drew an average attendance of more than 5,000.

We see significant differences between the megachurches today and these two examples mentioned from history. The Jerusalem church and Spurgeon's Tabernacle centered on biblical preaching and on calling for its members to be different from the world. Throughout the Old Testament the prophets called for the people of God to live holy lives and be distinct from the world. The New Testament writers did the same. The Apostle Paul called for holy and separate living in the lives of believers. *Do not be unequally yoked together with unbelievers. For what fellowship has righteousness with lawlessness? And what communion has light with darkness? And what accord has Christ with Belial? Or what part has a believer with an unbeliever? And what agreement has the temple of God with idols?*[269] The Apostle John echoed Paul's sentiments when he wrote, *Do not love the world or the things in the world. If anyone loves the world, the love of the Father is not in him. For all that is in the world—the lust of the flesh, the lust of the eyes, and the pride of life—is not of the Father but is of the world. And the world is passing away, and the lust of it; but he who does the will of God abides forever.*[270]

Charles Spurgeon's preaching also called for holy living. "Put your finger on any prosperous page in the church's history, and I will find a little marginal note reading thus: 'In this age men could readily see where the church began and where the world ended.' Never were there good times when the church and the world were joined in marriage. The more the church is different from the world in her acts and in her maxims, the more true is her testimony for Christ, and the more potent is her witness against sin."[271] For his entire ministry Spurgeon maintained that conviction. Years later he preached, "I believe that one reason why the church of God at this present moment has so little influence over the world is because the world has so much influence over the church."[272]

The modern megachurch has grown because some of her leaders have diluted doctrine and embraced cultural standards and styles. Their goal is to be sensitive to seekers and help them feel good about themselves. Pragmatism, not biblical orthodoxy, is their prevailing philosophy. Most of the megachurch practices are not counter-cultural but correspond to the culture. They are hip and trendy like the culture is. They are successful marketers to a consumer-driven culture. "Indeed, it may be that this largely explains the emergence of the megachurches. The expectations of the postwar baby boomers have been shaped by such a therapeutic bounty and surfeit of on-demand entertainment that small, struggling, one-dimensional churches may well appear unattractive and uninviting however real and faithful their worship and service may be."[273]

Without a doubt, the church is in transition today. Will this era bring about permanent change, or is this a temporary phase for the church? David Wells poses some interesting questions as well. "How is the church to confront the one god who now holds sway—the god of personal choice? How is the church to chart a course in a culture cut loose from the past, a culture defined only by the present . . .. What is the church to do when old patterns of reasoning appear to have gone the way of the dinosaur . . .? What is the church to do in a world that places a higher value on style than substance and on experience than truth?"274

The answer is not "blowing in the wind" but is bound within the Word of God. It involves going back to the basics of our faith to recover the authority of God's Word over every area of life. The answer is before us if we simply have "eyes to see." In the 1939 American film *The Wizard of Oz*, Dorothy, played by Judy Garland, searched all over the land of Oz for a better place "somewhere over the rainbow." After an eventful search she discovered her heart's desire was in her own backyard. Church leaders, young and old, have searched the mystical land of Oz and have not found that for which they are searching. "*And you will seek Me and find Me, when you search for Me with all your heart. I will be found by you, says the Lord, and I will bring you back from your captivity.*"275

ENDNOTES

Chapter 1

[1]Paul Lee Tan, *Encyclopedia of 7700 Illustrations* (Rockville: Assurance Publishers, 1982), 257.

[2]John Naisbitt, *Megatrends: Ten New Directions Transforming Our Lives* (New York: Warner Books Inc., 1982), 23.

[3]Joyce Howard Price, "Traditional Family Nowhere Near Extinct," *Washington Times*, May 28, 1998.

[4]Benton Johnson, Dean R. Hughes, and Donald A. Luidens, "Mainline Churches: The Real Reason for Decline," *First Things* 31 (March 1993): 13-18.

[5]Peter Smith, "Presbyterian Membership Decline Worsens" *The Courier-Journal,* June 22, 2008.

[6]Thom S. Rainer, *The Unchurched Next Door* (Grand Rapids: Zondervan, 2003). Rainer's research explodes many of the myths believed by pastors and church members.

[7]http://www.texasescapes.com/TexasGhostTowns/Little-Hope-Texas.htm (accessed September 11, 2008).

[8]Matthew 11:2-6

[9]George MacLeod, *Only One Way Left* (Glasgow: Iona Community, 1956), 38.

Chapter 2

[10]1 Kings 17:1

[11]1 Kings 18:17-18

[12]Jeremiah chapters 26-37

[13]Acts 16:16-24

[14]Colossians 2:8

[15]2 Thessalonians 2:15

[16] David F. Wells, *God in the Wasteland: The Reality of Truth in a World of Fading Dreams*, (Grand Rapids: William B. Eerdmans, 1994), 148-149.

[17]cf Romans 3:23; 6:23

[18]1 Corinthians 1:21

[19]"When You Are Asked to Give Public Prayer in a Diverse Society," The National Conference for Community and Justice http://www.nccjstl.org/resource/publicprayer.htm. (accessed September 11, 2008).

[20]ibid

[21]Colossians 2:11

[22]Paul Thigpen, "Ancient altars, Pentecostal fire," *Ministries Today*, Nov/Dec 1992, 42-51.

[23]James Kelly, *Current Thoughts and Trends* 14. April 1998, 20.

[24]Colossians 2:18-19

[25]Ruth M. Armstrong, "The Psychology of Inner and Outer Space," *Pastoral Psychology* 37 No 3 Spring 1989, 161-164.

[26]Colossians 2:20-23

[27]Leviticus 10:1-3

[28]see also Exodus 30:9

[29]John 4:24

Chapter 3

[30]Proverbs 23:23

[31]2 John 4

[32]Andy Crouch, "The Emergent Mystique," *Christianity Today* 48 No 11. November, 2004. 38.

[33]John MacArthur, *The Truth War: Fighting for Certainty in an Age of Deception* (Nashville, Thomas Nelson Publisher, 2007), 17.

[34]1 Timothy 3:15

[35]2 John 5-6

[36]Ibid

[37]1 Corinthians 13:6

[38]1 John 4:20

[39]2 John 7-9

[40]2 John 8

[41]David Roach, "CBF Presenter Questions Christ's Deity" *Baptist Press* June 19, 2008. http://bpnews.net/bpnews.asp?id=28326 (accessed September 11, 2008).

[42]2 John 10-11 – John is probably referring to hospitality that goes beyond mere greeting and including food and lodging.

Chapter 4

[43]William H. Willimon, "Answering Pilate: Truth and the Postliberal Church," *The Christian Century* 104, no. 3 (January 28 1987): 82-85.

[44]Ibid, 84

[45]Robert Bellah, *Habits of the Heart, Individualism and Commitment in American Life* (New York: Harper & Row Publishers, 1986), 84.

[46]The entire story is found in Acts 19:21-41.

[47]Acts 19:32, 39, 41. Here *ekklesia* is translated "assembly" referring to the secular gathering of this group in the theater.

[48]Acts 19:39

[49]Acts 19:41

[50]Acts 7:38

[51]Psalm 22:22 quoted in Hebrews 2:12

[52]Luke 7:5

[53]1 Timothy 3:15

[54]Acts 8:1

[55]Acts 13:1

[56]1 Corinthians 1:2

[57]Acts 9:31

[58]1 Corinthians 16:19

[59]Galatians 1:2

[60]Acts 14:23

[61]Philippians 4:15-16

[62]J.K Dagg, *Manual of Theology, Second Part* (Harrisonburg, VA: Baker Book House, 1990), 100.

[63]Carroll, B.H, *An Interpretation of the English Bible: Colossians, Ephesians, and Hebrews*, ed. J.B Cranfill (Grand Rapids: Baker Book House, 1948), 102.

[64]Robert L. Saucy, *The Church in God's Program* (Chicago: Moody Press, 1972), 17.

[65]This story was told to the author as a seminary student in 1977 at Mid-America Baptist Theological Seminary by a professor. Dr. R.G. Lee

was pastor at Bellevue Baptist for 33 years (1927-1960) and died in 1978.

[66]1 Corinthians 3:9

[67]1 Peter 2:10

[68]Ephesians 2:19

[69]Galatians 6:10

[70]Ephesians 5:22-32

[71]Ephesians 1:22-23

[72]Ephesians 5:22-33

[73]Ephesians 1:22-23; 1 Corinthians 12:12-27

[74]1 Timothy 3:15

Chapter 5

[75]Marc Howard, "Taking Care of Local Church Business," *Growing Churches* 7, no. 4 (Summer 1987): 13-14.

[76]Matthew 16:18

[77]Ephesians 5:25

[78]Hebrews 10:25

[79]The Apostles Creed and/or the Nicene Creed are broadly accepted denominationally. Baptists and Quakers, however, reject the authority of those creeds. Baptists have formulated their own Confessions of Faith.

[80]Galatians 6:2

[81]Hebrews 3:13

[82]1 Corinthians 12:25

[83]Acts 2:44-45

[84]Michael S. Horton, "All Crossed Up," *Touchstone*, March 2008, 13.

[85]Matthew 18:15-17

[86]1 Corinthians 5:1-13

[87]Acts 2:41

[88]Acts 5:1-11

[89]Acts 5:13

[90]Greek word *kollao* from *kolla* meaning "glue"

[91]1 Corinthians 6:16

[92]1 Timothy 3:1. The word *bishop* is from *episkope* and is an overseer.

[93]1 Timothy 3:5

Chapter 6

[94]Robert W. Patterson, "In Search of the Visible Church," *Christianity Today* 34, no. 3 (March 11 1991): 36-38.

[95]Bethlehem Baptist Church in Minneapolis, MN is an example of a strong Baptist Church that has conceded its historic position on baptism. Article III, Section 2, Paragraphs 4-5 reveal this change. http://desiring-god.org/media/pdf/baptism_and_membership.pdf. The evangelical world was stunned by this action

[96]Matthew 3:2-9; Acts 2:38

[97]Romans 6:2-4

[98]Acts 8:12-13a

[99]Acts 8:37-38

[100]Acts 9:1-19 is the story of Paul's conversion and baptism in vs. 18.

[101] Acts 10:47. When a person trusts in Christ for salvation, the Holy Spirit takes residence in that life.

[102] Acts 16:25-33

[103] Acts 18:8

[104] Acts 16:31-33

[105] Romans 6:4. The parentheses are mine for clarity and are not a part of the biblical text.

[106] Romans 6:5

[107] Acts 2:38

[108] The word *eis* is a primary preposition used figuratively as purpose or result. James Strong, "#1519 eis," in *A Concise Dictionary of the Words in the Greek New Testament*.

[109] Matthew 12:41. The same word *eis* is here translated "at"

[110] Joseph Henry Thayer, C. G. Grimm, and C. L. W. Wilke, "Baptizo," in *A Greek-English Lexicon of the New Testament (Abridged and Revised Thayer Lexicon)*

[111] Luther, Martin, *Works of Martin Luther The Philadelphia Edition*, trans. A.T.W Steinhaeuser, *Volume 2* (Philadelphia: Muhlenberg Press, 1943), 231.

[112] Calvin, John, *The Institutes of Christian Religion*, trans. Henry Beveridge (Grand Rapids: Christian Classics Ethereal Library, 2002), 2524, PDF http://www.ccel.org/ccel/calvin/institutes.pdf?membership_type=755f83dd5

a6c2741741740d30ebcc29679e3e2bd/ (accessed September 11, 2008).

113 John Wesley et al., *One Volume New Testament Commentary* (Grand Rapids: Baker Book House, 1957), Romans 6:4.

114 James Gibbons, *The Faith Of Our Fathers* (Baltimore: John Murphy & Co, 1877), 275.

115 A Great Commission is given in every Gospel (Mt 28:16-20; Mk 16:14-18; Lk 24:46-49; Jn 21:19-23) and in the book of Acts (1:4-8). The one most people refer to is Matthew 28:18-20.

116 Acts 8:26-38

117 Matthew 28:16

118 Mark 16:14

119 Luke 24:33

120 John 20:19

121 Colossians 1:28

122 2 Corinthians 5:20

123 J.L. Dagg, *Manual of Theology, Second Part*, Gano Books, 1982, p. 95.J.L Dagg, *Manual of Theology Second Part* (Harrisonburg, VA: Gano Books, 1990), 95.

Chapter 7

124 Matthew 28:19

125 Matthew 16:18

126 1 Corinthians 3:11

127 Ephesians 2:20

128 1 Corinthians 12:28

129 Merrill F. Unger, "Apostle," in *Unger's Bible Dictionary*, 1957 ed.

130 Acts 1:21-22

131 Matthew 28:18

132 Isaiah 7:14 is quoted in Matthew 1:23

133 Matthew 28:19, 20a

134 Romans 10:13-15a

135 Franklin Hamlin Littlel, *The Anabaptist View of Church*, 2nd ed. (Boston: Star King Press, 1958), 114.

136 ibid, p. 114

137 Matthew 28:19

[138] Mark 1:10-11. This account is also in Matthew 3:16-17 and Luke 3:22

[139] Matthew 28:20, parentheses mine.

[140] 2 Timothy 3:16-17

[141] Jesus quoted Deuteronomy 8:3 and recorded in Luke 4:4.

[142] Acts 20:27

Chapter 8

[143] "Wrath of the Green Ants," *Time Magazine*, September 9, 2008, *www.time.com/time/magazine/article/0,9171,904108,00.html.* (accessed September 11, 2008).

[144] Isaiah 29:14 quoted in 1 Corinthians 1:19

[145] 1 Corinthians 1:27, 29

[146] In Acts 17:16 "given over to idols" is translated from *kateidoolos*. It is only used here in the New Testament.

[147] Deuteronomy 32:6; Psalm 106:29; Isaiah 65:3

148 Acts 17:16

[149] Alexander, Joseph Addison, *The Acts of the Apostles, Volume II* (New York: Charles Scribner & Co., 1869), 145.

[150] W.J. Conybeare and J.S. Howson, *The Life and Epistles of St Paul* (Grand Rapids: Wm. B. Eerdmans, 1999), 280.

[151] W. E. Vine, "Encounter," in *A Comprehensive Dictionary of the Original Greek Words with their Precise English Meanings*, 1990 ed, 366.

[152] David Roach, "Faith healer Todd Bentley separates from wife, draws criticism from charismatics," *Baptist Press*, August 19 2008, http://www.bpnews.net/bpnews.asp?id=28727/ (accessed September 11, 2008).

[153] Ecclesiastes 1:9

[154] Acts 17:18

[155] Acts 17:24

[156] Acts 17:25b

[157] Acts 17:26b–27a

[158] Acts 17:30-31a

[159] John 16:5-11

[160] Romans 10:9-10

Chapter 9

161 George Barna, *The Barna Report 1994-1995 Virtual America* (Ventura California: Regal Books, 1994), 78.

162 Revelation 3:15-16

163 William Willimon, "A Crisis of Identity," *Sojourners* 15, no. 5 (May 1986): 24.

164 1 John 2:15-16

165 1 Timothy 5:23

166 1 Timothy 4:12

167 These times were described in 2 Timothy 3:1-7

168 2 Timothy 4:3-4

169 In the pastoral epistles, Paul refers to "truth" 5 times in his first letter to Timothy (2:4,7; 3:15; 4:3; 6:5), 6 times in 2 Timothy (2:15,18,25; 3:7-8; 4:4), and 2 times to Titus (1:1,14).

170 John MacArthur, *The Truth War: Fighting for Certainty in an Age of Deception* (Nashville: Thomas Nelson, 2007), xxiii.

171 Proverbs 22:28

172 J. Robert Wright, Editor, *Ancient Christian Commentary on Scripture: Proverbs, Ecclesiastes, Song of Solomon*, Vol IX, (Downers Grove: InterVarsity, 2005) 143.

173 2 Timothy 1:7

174 2 Timothy 2:25-26

175 2 Timothy 1:13

176 2 Timothy 3:14

177 2 Timothy 4:2

178 2 Timothy 3:15-16

179 "Inspiration" is translated from the Greek word *theopneustos* and means "God breathed." The Jews in Paul's day virtually took this truth for granted.

180 Russell D. Moore, "Evangelical Theological Society rejects 'open theism,' affirms God's foreknowledge," *Baptist Press*, Nov 20, 2001. http://www.bpnews.net/bpnews.asp?Id=12210/ (accessed September 11, 2008).

181 David Neff, "Dispatch from Atlanta: What Fireworks?" *Christianity Today* 47 (Nov 1, 2003). http://www.christianitytoday.com/ct/2003/novemberweb-only/11-17-

41.0.html/ (accessed September 11, 2008).

[182] 2 Timothy 4:5

[183] Proverbs 11:30

[184] 2 Corinthians 5:10-11a

[185] 2 Timothy 4:7

Chapter 10

[186] 1 Thessalonians 3:2b-3a

[187] 2 Thessalonians 2:2

[188] 2 Thessalonians 2:15

[189] Matthew 7:24-27

[190] 1 Thessalonians 1:6

[191] 1 Thessalonians 3:2-4

[192] 2 Thessalonians 2:2-3a

[193] 1 Corinthians 10:12-13

[194] 2 Thessalonians 2:5

[195] 2 Thessalonians 2:15

[196] Strong, #4739

[197] Paul's admonition is found in 2 Thessalonians 2:1-17, the falling away in vs. 3 and stand fast in vs. 15.

[198] Strong, #646

[199] Charlotte Allen, "Liberal Christianity is paying for its sins" *Los Angeles Times* July 9, 2006. http://articles.latimes.com/2006/jul/09/opinion/op-allen9 (accessed September 11, 2008).

[200] ibid

[201] ibid

[202] 2 Peter 3:4

[203] John 14:6

[204] Acts 4:12

[205] Bishop Joseph Sprague, "Affirmations of a Dissenter," interview by Iliff School of Theology (Denver, Co, June 25, 2002), *Methodist Church.com* (Summer 2002), ASP http://www.themethodistchurch.com/Sprague.asp/ (accessed September 11, 2008).

[206] 2 Thessalonians 3:15

[207] 2 Thessalonians 2:16-17

Chapter 11

[208] Isaiah 40:3

[209] Malachi 3:1

[210] Luke 3:19

[211] Matthew 3:7-12

[212] Matthew 3:5

[213] John 3:27-30

[214] William R. Estep, *The Anabaptist Story* (Grand Rapids: William B. Eerdmans, 1975), 51-71.

[215] John Foxe, *Foxe's Christian Martyrs of the World* (Chicago: Moody Press), 218.

[216] Matthew 3:5-6

[217] Mark 6:20

[218] Mark 6:17-28

[219] Matthew 11:11

[220] John 1:19

[221] Tom Nettles, *The Baptists: Key People Involved in Forming a Baptist Identity*, Vol 1 (Fearn, Ross-shire: Christian Focus Publications), 62.

[222] 1 Corinthians 14:7-8

[223] John 1:20-23

[224] Ed Stetzer, "Church Planting and Survivability," *Research Reflections* (Center for Missional Research, North American Mission Board, Feb 2007).

[225] J.M. Frost, *Baptist Why and Why Not* (Nashville: Broadman & Holman, 1996), 3.

[226] John 1:6-8

[227] David F. Wells, *God in the Wasteland: The Reality of Truth in a World of Fading Dreams* (Grand Rapids: William B. Eerdmans, 1994), 147.

[228] D. Martyn Lloyd-Jones, *Preaching and Preachers* (Grand Rapids: Zondervan, 1971), 105.

[229] Isaiah 6:1-13

[230] Jeremiah 1:1-10

[231] Ezekiel 2:1-10

[232] John 1:20-21

[233] John 1:23

[234] Peter Leithart, "What's Wrong with Evangelical Theology," *First Things* 65, (August/September 1996), 19-21. http://www.leaderu.com/ftissues/ft9608/opinion/leithart.html (accessed September 18, 2008)

[235] ibid

[236] David F. Wells, *God in the Wasteland: The Reality of Truth in a World of Fading Dreams*, (Grand Rapids: William B. Eerdmans, 1994), 84.

[237] John 1:25

[238] David F. Wells, *The Courage to Be Protestant: Truth-lovers, Marketers, and Emergents in the Postmodern World* (Grand Rapids: William B. Eerdmans, 2008), 11.

[239] 2 Peter 1:20-21

[240] Malcolm B. Yarnell, III, "Changing Baptist Concepts of Royal Priesthood: John Smyth and Edgar Young Mullins, *The Rise of the Laity in Evangelical Protestantism* (New York: Routledge, 2002), 248.

[241] Matthew 3:2

[242] Matthew 3:8-10 (check to be sure this is right verse)

Chapter 12

[243] Donald E. Miller, *Reinventing American Protestantism: Christianity in the New Millennium* (Berkeley: University of California Press, 1997), 4.

[244] Romans 12:2a

[245] Romans 12:2b

[246] 1 Peter 1:14. The Greek word *suschematizo* J.H. Merle d'Aubign

[247] James Davidson Hunter, *American Evangelicalism: Conservative Religion and the Quandary of Modernity* (New Brunswick: Rutgers University Press, 1983), 129-130.

[248] Reggie McNeal, *The Present Future: Six Tough Questions for the Church* (San Francisco: Jossey-Bass, 2003), xvi.

[249] ibid, 4.

[250] Ephesians 5:25

[251] Reggie McNeal, *The Present Future: Six Tough Questions for the Church* (San Francisco: Jossey-Bass, 2003), xvi.

[252] Ibid, 4

[253] 1 Corinthians 1:21

[254] Matthew 4:17

[255] David Mills, "Preaching Without Reaching: The Irrelevance of Relevant Preaching," *Touchstone: A Journal of Mere Christianity* 20, no 6 (July/August 2007): 26.

[256] ibid, p.25

[257] Andy Crouch, "The Emergent Mystique," *Christianity Today* 48 no. 11, (November 2004), *http://www.christianitytoday.com/ct/2004/november/12.36.html* (accessed September 24, 2008).

[258] ibid

[259] Psalm 29:2

[260] Psalm 95:6

[261] John 4:24

[262] Amos 5:22-23

[263] Psalm 51:16-17

[264] John 4:20

[265] C. H. Spurgeon, *No Compromise in Metropolitan Tabernacle Pulpit*, Vol. 34 (Pasadena: Pilgrim Publications, 1974), 560.

[266] Psalm 30:4

[267] J.H. Merle d'Aubigné

[268] The research in this survey was done by Leadership Network (www.leadnet.org) and Hartford Institute for Religion Research at the Hartford Seminary (http//hirr.hartsem.edu).

[269] 2 Corinthians 6:14-16a

[270] 1 John 2:15-17

[271] C. H. Spurgeon, *Separating the Precious From the Vile in The New Park Street Pulpit*, Vol. 6 (Pasadena: Pilgrim Publications, 1981), p 154.

[272] C. H. Spurgeon, *How to Become Fishers of Men in Metropolitan Tabernacle* Pulpit, Vol. 32 (Pasadena: Pilgrim Publications, 1974), 339.

[273] David F. Wells, *God in the Wasteland* (Grand Rapids: William B. Eerdmans, 1994), 74.

[274] ibid, p. 221.

[275] Jeremiah 29:13-14a

Order more copies of

The Vanishing Church

Call toll free: 1-800-747-0738

Visit: *www.hannibalbooks.com*

Email: *orders@hannibalbooks.com*

FAX: 1-888-252-3022

Mail copy of form below to:

Hannibal Books

P.O. Box 461592

Garland, Texas 75046

Number of copies desired _____

Multiply number of copies by $ 14.95

Sub-total _____

Please add $4 for postage and handling for first book and add $1.00 for each additional book in the order.

Shipping and handling$_____

Texas residents add 8.25% sales tax $_____

Total order $_____

Mark method of payment:

check enclosed _____

Credit card# _____

exp. date_____ (Visa, MasterCard, Discover, American Express accepted)

Name _____

Address _____

City State, Zip _____

Phone _____ FAX _____

Email _____

Notes

<u>Notes</u>

Notes

1760584

Made in the USA